Family and Human Capital in Turkish Migration

TRANSNATIONAL PRESS LONDON

Turkish Migration Series

Family and Human Capital in Turkish Migration, 2ⁿᵈ Ed.

Conflict, Insecurity & Mobility

Politics and Law in Turkish Migration

Göç ve Uyum

Family and Human Capital in Turkish Migration

2nd Edition

Editors:

Nadja **Milewski**

Ibrahim **Sirkeci**

M. Murat **Yüceşahin**

Assia S. **Rolls**

Editorial Assistant: Therese **Svensson**

TRANSNATIONAL PRESS LONDON

2015

Family and Human Capital in Turkish Migration, 2nd Edition

Edited by Nadja Milewski, Ibrahim Sirkeci, M. Murat Yüceşahin, Assia S. Rolls

First Printing: 2015

Paperback

ISBN 978-1-910781-16-6

Cover Photo: Mansi THAKKER

TRANSNATIONAL PRESS LONDON
12 Ridgeway Gardens, London, N6 5XR, United Kingdom
www.tplondon.com

For families of guest workers

Contents

Acknowledgements

Academic publishing is paddling through a challenging environment while academics are under increasing pressure to produce output. Edited volumes are rather difficult to come about and the process requires input from so many parties. Therefore we would like to thank all our colleagues who have contributed to this volume, those who have participated at the *Turkish Migration Conference 2014* at *Regent's University London*, as well as many others who have volunteered to review the papers for the conference and for the edited book. All these efforts combined made this book possible. We also thank to colleagues at *Regent's University London* and *Ria Financial*, and *Migration Letters* journal for their generous and constant support. We thank *Therese Svensson* for her thorough work in copy-editing the manuscript. We thank *Transnational Press London* editors and production team. Finally, our families and friends deserve a thank you for their continuous support.

About the authors

Dr Birgit Becker is an associate professor of Sociology with a Focus on Empirical Educational Research at Goethe University Frankfurt, Department of Sociology, and member of the Center for Research on Individual Development and Adaptive Education of Children at Risk (IDeA). Her research interests are education and educational inequality, early childhood and socialization, and the integration of immigrants.

Nicole Biedinger is a project consultant at the GESIS-Leibniz Institute for the Social Sciences, Mannheim, Germany. Her main research interests include social and ethnic inequalities in early abilities of children and early educational inequalities as well as early educational decisions.

Işık Kulu-Glasgow is a researcher at the Research and Documentation Centre (WODC) of the Dutch Ministry of Security and Justice, in The Hague. She has been involved in various research projects on migration, asylum and integration issues, and published on the topic nationally and internationally. Her research interests involve immigration policy, family/marriage migration, labour migration, and integration and integration policy. Her recent publications in English include "Restricting Turkish marriage migration? National policy, couples' coping strategies and international obligations" (*Migration Letters*, 2013, with A. Leerkes); "Categorical accommodation and assistance for victims of trafficking in human beings" (WODC, 2012, with AM. Galloway, EMT Beenakkers, M. Smit and F. Zwenk); "Playing Hard(er) to Get: The State, International Couples, and the Income Requirement" (*European Journal of Migration and Law* 13, 2011 with A. Leerkes).

Jörg Hartmann studied Sociology, Mathematics, and Business Studies at the University of Leipzig, Germany. Since 2009, he has worked as a research assistant at the Georg-August-University of Göttingen, Germany, currently writing his PhD thesis. His research interests include migration, integration, social stratification research, and quantitative methods. Motivated by his interest in understanding the mechanisms of migrant assimilation, his Phd project focuses on Germany's second-generation migrants and the labour market disadvantages they experience over the course of their career.

Dr Doreen Huschek is a researcher at the Department of Criminology at Stockholm University. She works on issues relating to behaviors over the life course such as union formation and partnership formation of migrants and offending and its reciprocal relation with demographic behaviors. Her PhD at the Netherlands Interdisciplinary Demographic Institute (NIDI) compared the partnership behavior of children of Turkish migrants in several European countries and focused on the influence of parents, peers and institutions.

Dr Johanna Kint has a background in art history (KULeuven). She worked on a PhD research project at the Delft University of Technology. She coaches and teaches at Bachelor and Master's level at the TU/e and at LUCA campus Brussels. Her research focuses on socio-cultural issues in relation to the multicultural neighborhood of Brussels. She is aware of the fact that the lack of solutions for the complexities of the modern world – i.e. environmental issues, cultural clashes and the breakdown of cultures – indicates that Western society touches on the limits of positivism and rational thinking. Her concern goes to mutual respect and appreciation as a basic attitude to cultural dialogue and understanding. This reflection on action in an intercultural context is what she considers to be our new language.

Oliver Klein is a researcher at the Mannheim Centre for European Social Research (MZES) at the University of Mannheim, Germany. His research interests include child development as well as social and ethnic inequalities in the educational system and labor market.

Sietske Klooster graduated in 2003 at the faculty of Industrial Design Engineering of the University of Technology in Delft. Here she started to develop her own design approach during her graduation project 'design moves'. She further developed this approach in close cooperation with the faculty of Industrial Design of the TU Eindhoven, focusing on Choreography of Interaction. Her next step of development moved her into the combination of farm and city life, where food was incorporated in her embodied design work. Here the design-choreography of food production and consumption became her core business. Currently the project 'The MilkSalon' is running as a case study, to fine-tune, represent and illustrate her design principles.

Prof Dr Beatrice Knerr is a professor at the University of Kassel (Germany) where she heads the Department of Development Economics, Migration and Agricultural Policy (DEMAP). She holds a PhD degree from Kiel University and received her habilitation from the University of Stuttgart, Hohenheim. Her research priorities are economic development in low-income countries, labour mobility and rural development. Among her publications are ten monographs and edited and co-edited books, and almost 100 articles and book chapters in these areas, around half of them on labor migration and mobility.

Prof Dr Stephan Letzel graduated in engineering and medicine. In 1988 he obtained his medical license and doctorate. He received his habilitation in 1994 from the medical faculty in Erlangen. Today, Professor Stephan Letzel is director of the Institute of Occupational, Social and Environmental Medicine (since 2001) and of the Institute for Teacher Health (since 2011), both part of the University Medical Center of the Johannes Gutenberg-University Mainz. There he teaches social medicine, public health and occupational medicine. Research foci are in the range of toxicity agents and occupational malignancies. His extramural activities include, among other things, being Chairman of the Ethics Commission of the State Medical Association Rhineland-Palatinate.

Dr Nadja Milewski is an Assistant Professor of Demography at the University of Rostock, Germany, Institute for Sociology and Demography. Her research centers on demographic behavior and life courses of international migrants, and their integration into Western European host societies. Nadja Milewski was a doctoral student at the Max Planck Institute for Demographic Research Rostock and worked at the Institut National d'Etudes Démographiques, Paris. She has worked as a research scientist at the University of Rostock since 2009.

Dr Öncel Naldemirci is researcher at the Department of Sociology, University of Gothenburg. He currently works at the same department and takes part in a research project, *The Challenges of Translating Person-Centred Care from Theory into Practice*. He holds a PhD in Sociology from the University of Gothenburg (Sweden) and a BA and MA from Boğaziçi University (Turkey). His main areas of research are migration, care, ageing and emotions. His PhD thesis, *Caring (in) Diaspora* investigated ageing experiences and care expectations of older Turkish people in a Swedish context.

Maja Richtermoc is MA of German Sciences and Turcology. She graduated in 2014 at the Faculty of Humanities and Social Sciences (University of Zagreb) in the field of cultural studies, focusing on integration and identity issues of citizens with Turkish migration backgrounds. She is currently working as a language teacher and translator for German and Turkish language. She regularly takes part in conferences and summer schools in the fields of her interest. She intends to intensify her scientific activities in the fields of linguistics and comparative cultural and political studies. Her research is centered on socio-political and socio-cultural transitions in the region and Europe, minority issues and sociolinguistics.

Dr Assia Rolls is currently Head of Research and Professional Development in the Regent's Institute of Language and Culture. Assia's research interests lie in classroom second language acquisition, teacher education and teacher development. She, has, for many years, researched the relationship between language learning and teaching and what learners get out of the classroom. Her interest in traditional academic classroom-centred research has more recently shifted towards teacher and learner development via the notion of 'Exploratory Practice', a form of practitioner research involving teachers and learners working together to foster a better understanding of their learning and teaching environment. She has written and reported on her work in national and international fora. Working in the multicultural environment of Regent's University, Assia has also developed an interest in internationalisation of the curriculum and transnational studies. She is the associate director of Regent's Centre for Transnational Studies and the Editor of *Border Crossing Transnational Working Papers*.

Prof Dr Ibrahim Sirkeci is Ria Financial Professor of Transnational Studies and Marketing and the Director of the Regent's Centre for Transnational Studies (RCTS) at Regent's University London (UK). He holds a PhD in Geography from the University of Sheffield (UK) and a BA in Political Science and Public Administration from Bilkent University (Turkey). Prior to joining Regent's University London, Sirkeci had worked at the University of Bristol. His main areas of expertise are Human Mobility, Transnational Marketing and Consumers, Marketing of Business Schools, Labour Markets, Remittances, and Segmentation. He is the editor of several journals including *Migration Letters* and *Transnational Marketing Journal*. His books include *Transnational Marketing and Transnational Consumers* (Springer, 2013), *Migration and Remittances during the Global Financial Crisis and Beyond* (World Bank, 2012 with J. Cohen and D. Ratha), and *Cultures of Migration, the global nature of contemporary mobility* (University of Texas Press, 2011 with J. Cohen) which was named 'Outstanding Academic Title' by Choice magazine in the USA. He has been chairing the *Turkish Migration Conference* series since 2012.

Dr Ulaş Sunata is Assistant Professor in Department of Sociology at Bahçeşehir University, İstanbul, Turkey. Dr Sunata obtained her PhD in Sociology at University of Osnabrück, Germany where she has worked as a Guest Fellow at Institut für Migrationsforschung und Interkulturelle Studien (IMIS). She holds a Master of Science in Sociology and Bachelor of Arts in Statistics, both from Middle East Technical University (METU), Ankara, Turkey. Her research interests include information society, nationalism, migration and gender studies, on which she has published several articles and two books. She is the author of *Highly Skilled Labor Migration: The Case Study of ICT Specialists from Turkey in Germany*. Berlin, Münster: LIT Verlag (2011) and *Not a "Flight" from Home, But 'Potential Brain Drain'*. Saarbrücken: VDM Verlag Dr. Müller (2010).

Dr Rebecca Tlatlik studied Political Science and Cultural Anthropology at the University of Göttingen, Germany. After completing her studies in 2010, she started working as a Research assistant in the Department of Development Policy, Migration and Agricultural Policy (DEMAP) at the University of Kassel. There she was in charge of seminars and lectures to Bachelor and Master students in development economics and labour migration. Her PhD project focuses on the staying intention of international students in the city of their studies. During her doctoral work she obtained advanced knowledge in quantitative and qualitative social research methods and presented her work at several international conferences. Her research interests are international student migration, migration policy, the internationalization of higher education and regional economic policy.

Dr M. Murat Yüceşahin is an associate professor at Ankara University, Faculty of Language and History-Geography, Department of Geography, Turkey. After received his PhD from the Institute of Social Sciences at Ankara University in 2002, Dr Yüceşahin's major research interest focused on population geography. In 2011, as a collaborator researcher, Dr Yüceşahin participated to the World Population Programme at the International Institute for Applied Systems Analysis (IIASA), Laxenburg, Austria and worked on Turkey's fertility, mortality and migration trends and sub national level population projection. His current research primarily focuses on population geography, social geography and feminist geography. Besides serving as ad hoc reviewer and editorial board member for journals including *Migration Letters*, Dr Yüceşahin is a managing editor of the international peer-reviewed Turkish journal of migration, *Göç Dergisi*.

Ulrike Zier studied sociology and Islamic studies in Bamberg and Paris between 2003 and 2009 with a focus on sociology of migration and interethnic relations as well as European studies. Since 2009 Ulrike Zier is a research assistant at the Institute of Occupations, Social and Environmental Medicine of the University Medical Center of the Johannes Gutenberg University Mainz. There she teaches social medicine, public health and occupational medicine. Since 2013 she leads the working group of social medicine and public health. Main topics of research are relations of over-indebtedness and poverty to health, migrant's health and health care utilization.

Introduction: Family and demography in Turkish mobility

M. Murat Yüceşahin, Nadja Milewski, Ibrahim Sirkeci, Assia S. Rolls

What we like about the concept of this book is that it brings together findings of one origin group at several destinations and shows several aspects of the incorporation processes of the group and the life courses of individuals. It does less center on the effect of the receiving contexts, but rather highlights parallels of the same group in different countries and in Turkey. Thus, perhaps our presentation is overcoming some of methodological nationalism common to migration studies. Thereby allowing to get an impression of the variety of Turkish migrants' life in Western Europe, where you cannot draw a simple picture of black and white as may current public integration debates suggest. Attempts of "integration" or multicultural societies have not either failed or have been successful overall; it is rather certain areas where multicultural co-existence with the neighbours of the majority populations works out. In some other areas, vulnerability and disadvantages of the immigrant group are prominent.

In any case, Turkish immigrants and their descendants in Western Europe are challended in integrating into their host countries and so are the majority populations. Not only culturally different but pionner Turkish immigrants in Europe were also socio-demographically distinct from the host societies. The socio-demographic distance – despite intergenerational upward mobility – somewhat continued to today.

Highest levels of human mobility is seen in some of the advanced economies in the "North" including Australia, Canada, and the United States. Main reason behind this is that some of these countries were established or significantly altered by large influxes of populations as these countries were territorially large and entertain less pressure on housing and employment as well as the presence of established cultures of migration. Thus internal and international mobility is higher in these new countries (See Newbold, 2010).

According to the United Nations, international migrants comprised around 3% of the world's population today. The expectation is that international human mobility is likely to rise even further in the near future. Many source countries of the past, such as Turkey are becoming significant destination countries as seen in the cases of Spain, Italy and Greece. In general industrial or many developed countries of the world are now experiencing immigration, even if they have yet come to view themselves as immigration countries (Brown and Bean, 2006: 347-348).

Economic, political, cultural, communal, individual, and familial conflicts (including disagreements, latent tensions, etc) are leading people to move. Those more capable and with means and support do move internally and internationally depending on human and social capitals and the severity of insecurity they perceive (Sirkeci, 2009). Thus migration is a function of conflict in broader sense. Turkey as a country suffered from major violent armed conflicts in recent history and a country in a region where wars never ending is likely to be a magnet of population movements.

Initiation of human movement and the destination choices are often determined by cultures of migration, conflicts (push factors) at the origin, moderating effects of social and human capital, and existing networks among individuals, countries, regions and so on (Sirkeci and Cohen, 2015). Across time and space, motivations, patterns of human movement vary but there are some regularities too. For example, differential rates regarding stages in the life cycle or age, employment patterns, ethnic and religious belonging, and other affiliations have an impact. Migrants are self-selected by subjective perception of the environments they live in and it can be said that migration is not a norm but an exception (Martin and Sirkeci, 2015). Movers are often healthy adults in working ages (Brown and Bean, 2006; Yaukey, 2007). Among movers, unmarried are more likely to appear, while families tend to move when they don't have children or when the children are young. Movers often come from groups of disadvantaged people at the countries of origin and they seek better jobs and opportunities despite being poor and less educated with limited resources to enable them to move (Brown and Bean, 2006: 349).

People with not the poorest backgrounds but those at lower middle classes and those from areas with mid level socio-economic development are more likely to move as they are expected to benefit from the move more than others (Sirkeci et al., 2012). Referring to the cultures of migration model, many labour migrants come from migrant households whose standard of living is often above subsistence levels but their sense of relative deprivation is stronger than others (Cohen and Sirkeci, 2011; Brown and Bean, 2006; Stark and Taylor, 1989).

It can be said that there is a gender balance among international movers across the world (Brown and Bean, 2006: 349). In certain parts of the world though, male labour migrants or female migrants dominate the flows of population for various reasons. Among mass movers often following violent major conflicts, gender balance is ensured while domestic worker flows, for example, in the Gulf countries is dominated by female workers. At the same time, contract migrants in many Arab countries almost exclusively attract men.

Population change features such as mortality and fertility is part and parcel of migration debate. Thus through migration these trends of fertility and mortality are moderated (White and Lindstrom, 2006; Rowland, 2012). Population movement is probably the most repeated and less predictable demographic event (Yaukey et al., 2007: 324). Nevertheless, human mobility is often the most debated element of the population change in many countries of destination.

Human mobility, by nature, leads to an increase in population at the countries of destination while having an adverse effect on the countries of origin which are often characterised by high fertility. Age selectivity and differential fertility are common features in these patterns. Such flows obviously affect the labour force sizes in the

3

countries involved in population movement. Selectivity by gender, age, health, and employment are also common features of this exchange of populations. Along with human mobility, there are finance, goods and culture flows in the form of social and material remittances (Sirkeci et al., 2012).

Newbold argues that most researchers agree that individuals or households migrate to improve their living conditions while each and every theory focuses on different aspects including economics, politics, culture, and environment (Newbold, 2010). Cohen and Sirkeci (2011) combine these into a culture of migration with conflict model.

As mentioned above, the most important demographic determinant of human mobility is probably age as population movements often dominated by young individuals (Newbold, 2010: 137). However, we are far from being able to predict the likelihood of human mobility by age as there are more complex patterns and embeddedness characterised by community, household, family and so on. Nevertheless, migration rates tend to increase among late teens and the early twenties. Elderly people, despite significant retirement flows present in certain parts of the world, do not move as often as the youth. Such age effect can also be attributed to life-cycle changes (Newbold, 2010: 137). Within human capital theory, migration rates can be explained by age too as young adults having a longer career time to recoup the costs of moving than older individuals. However, same trend can be said that more educated people have more resources to facilitate migration across borders. They also have wider networks and human capital to mobilise. There is a link between levels of education and long-distance human mobility.

Demographic factors, including gender, marital status, and the presence of children are correlates for human mobility. As mentioned above, gender balance is observed in certain flows but not in all. Single individuals are more likely to move longer distances when they are young, as family movement is often more costly and difficult; such moves often involves one partner's job relocation (Boyle et al., 2003).

Schooling needs also moderate migration of families (Newbold, 2010: 139).

Demographic transition debates have missed human mobility for a long while. The relationships between migration of particular groups and fertility transition or birth rate can be investigated. It would be important to remember here the classical two hypotheses about migration and the demographic transition nexus. Friedlandertakes a more classical approach in which fertility, mortality and migration are perceived as closely linked (Rowland, 2006: 391) whilst Zelinsky's approach focusing on population mobility ignores the relationship between migration, fertility, and mortality. Nevertheless, within the current scholarly debate of demographic transition, human mobility needs to be considered as a key feature. For example, fertility decline timing can be dependent on the availability of migration opportunities (Rowland, 2006: 391). It is possible to find a powerful link between these changes and the stages of the demographic transition in various parts of the World.

The family's central role in Turkey and among Turkish diaspora populations cannot be denied. The families of migrants residing in Western Europe often include second, third and even the forth generation of movers. Continuing flows of people from Turkey, often related to marriage and family formation, lead to creation of new first generation of movers. This creates dual or multiple levels and waves of integration processes as claimed by both new and old generations of migration scholarship. Intense migration movements from Turkey to western European countries and vice versa have led to border-crossing migration systems and transnational social spaces, where family relations are a key element (Pries, 2010).

Overall, family orientation is rather strong in Turkey. Main characteristics of the family system are strong intergenerational ties, which are expressed in emotional closeness, functional solidarity, and social control (Nauck & Suckow, 2002; Karakaşoğlu, 2012). In the context of international migration, the relationships between families and generations may change due to spatial distance to the family in the country of origin, processes of modernization (mainly education), and economic independence of family members (Nauck, 1985, 2001).

Previous research suggested both the families as a resource and therefore a protection in migration and integration processes as well as a source for conflicts between the generations which may even lead to a deterioration of individual health (Sluzki, 1971). Recent studies that compare families living in Turkey with transnational families, however, did not find evidence of conflict and disruption (e.g. Baykara-Krumme, 2013). They rather suggest that the migration context reinforces intergenerational relationships as compared to families living in Turkey, whereby spatial separation, naturally, reduces the frequency of personal contacts. At the same time, processes of acculturation in the host countries take place, which can mainly be observed in changing attitudes of the younger generation: children are less willing to support the older generation when the welfare state offers resources or when gender roles are changing, e.g., when women's labor-force participation increases (Milewski, 2013).

Compared to the respective host populations, Turkish families still show a higher degree of intergenerational support. They are able to combine traditional elements of Turkish culture and structural integration in the West. The integenerational ties and support appear as potential for the demographic aging of the Turkish population which will take place in the next decades.

The aging process and health of immigrants deserves pecial attention in research: Because 1) there appears different cultural understanding and perception of health and disease, 2) again, socio-economic disadvantages of the group relate to health disadvantages and differences in health behavior and disadvantages in the usage of health and care facilities, 3) the migration process and the experiences of discrimination and other difficulties related to migration and integration affect the health status of immigrants directly, 4) cultural and religious traditions may require health and health care practices in institutions for the elderly that differ from that of the majority population.

6

Research on health of international migrants is inconclusive. Studies focusing on younger or elderly migrants pointed out, sometimes contradicting results. However, it is argued that lower morbidity is observed among immigrants which is possibly linked to the selectivity of migration process as healthier and more able people are more likely to migrate compared to others. There are also other studies indicating that return migration tendency is higher among those migrants with illnesses (i.e. the salmon bias hypothesis) whereas some others refer to the health transition hypothesis (Razum & Twardella, 2002). Nevertheless, socio-economic status of immigrants on average is lower than that of the native born in destination countries. This structural disadvantage may lead to a gradual decline in health advantage immigrants arrive with at the beginning.

The aging processes of the Turkish population will be accompanied by a worse physical health status and an increasing care demand (Carnein et al., 2015). Mental health was found to be below average (Milewski & Doblhammer, 2015), and Turkish migrants more often said that they suffered from loneliness than non-migrants (Fokkema & Naderi, 2013).

Another area where we find a combination of traditional elements of a Turkish culture and Western modifications is marriage behavior and family formation among subsequent migrant generations. The second generation in this respect is in a special position as their parents come from societies in which the transition to adulthood often had and has other characteristics than is the case in north-western Europe. In many (in particular less industrialized) countries of origin of migrants the transition to adulthood takes place at younger ages, it follows a more standard sequence and is determined by norms on the timing and order of events in the life courese. Whereas the more patrilineal orientation in Turkey rather emphasizes gender roles according to the male-breadwinner model, members of the second migrant generation share more often egalitarian values as their parents' generation and show changes in gender role behaviour, for example, growing female labor force participation (e.g. Bernhardt & Goldscheider, 2007; Milewski, 2010).

It seems that the more the socio-economic structure of immigrants and their descendants resembles that of the host population, the more similar their family formation and fertility patterns will be. The number of children, eg, is smaller in second-generation families than it is among the first generation and in Turkey. The ages at union formation and at first childbearing have increased. By contrast, marriage remains the dominant living arrangement in the second generation, and marriage is strongly connected to a first child, ie, a marriage is only "complete" when a child has been born (Straßburger, 2003, Milewski, 2007, Yavuz, 2008).

The concept of human capital, needs mentioning at this junction, as it is used to analyse a wide range of aspects amongst them politics, economics, health, migration, innovation and evidently education, which features prominently in this spectrum. Human capital is viewed as the sum of skills and knowledge that people achieve through education and training. These knowledge and skills will enhance their productivity at work. This enhanced productivity brings in return a higher salary to the individual since a person's wage is likely to be conditioned by the person's productive capacity. As a result, people would invest in education to ensure that the private benefit equals the investment into the private costs of education. Hence higher the human capital the higher the (expected) returns on migration. Turkish migration has not been historically dominated by high skilled movers there are certain sub-flows where skilled movers are prominent.

In the opening chapter, Milewski and Huschek examine types and determinants of family involvement in marriages of second generation Turks in Western Europe. They investigate the ways in which partners meet and whether other family members have a stance on it. Their analysis covers 1320 women and men from Austria, Belgium, France, Germany, the Netherlands, Sweden, and Switzerland. Kint and Klooster reinterpret the cultural rituals around Turkish marriages. They approach the rituals with a dynamic understanding of the notion of culture which is constantly moving and changing.

Care at old age is a new challenge for Turkish immigrants in Europe and elsewhere. The two following chapters focus on this issue. Naldemirci studies the first-generation Turkish immigrants in Sweden who are now reaching older ages and thinking about their care needs. Strong family and community ties, intergenerational solidarity, and cultural practices regulating marriage, socialization and care are believed to be characteristic of Turkish families. She focuses on the fact that migration brings changes. The way people understand and express creatively their emotions change with mobility. Zier and Letzel examine health care utilization as an important means of maintaining and restoring personal health with reference to cultural differences in Germany. Based on a cross sectional survey, they have screened two random samples, each containing 2.000 addresses of inhabitants aged between 20 and 65 years. They discuss the results to show the characteristics of those who participated in the study and the non-participants in both Turkish and German samples.

Human capital has received wide attention in migration literature almost irrespective of discipline. Biedinger, Becker and Klein focus on mother language ability of Turkish children in Germany. This is a rather understudied topic in the literature where a substantial number of works exist on immigrants' acquisition of the host country language. Their empirical analysis explores the role of contexts such as family, media, peers, on the acquisition of the heritage language by children. Then we turn our attention to two papers on highly skilled Turkish migrants in the Netherlands and Germany both looking at the government attempts to attract and challenges faced. Kulu-Glasgow draws attention to what she calls the global 'battle for brains'. Dutch government's policies to attract highly skilled migrants from outside the European Union are examined. Highly skilled Turkish immigrants and second generation Turks in the Netherlands are among the target groups, but Kulu-Glasgow asks the crucial question of should I stay or should I go by focusing on factors behind different mobility intentions

9

with reference to the value-expectancy model of De Jong and Fawcett (1981). Tlatlik and Knerr investigated the changing pattern of highly skilled migration flows between Germany and Turkey with reference to Germany's need for high skilled people. Their question is how to keep Turkish graduates with German degrees in Germany to match the need for high skilled labour.

Richtermoc and Hartman offer us two chapters with focus on integration and career mobility. Richtermoc's case study illustrates the identity formation processes among young Austrians with Turkish migration background in Vienna. The ways in which multiple identities are created over Turkish and Austrian socio-cultural values and knowledge in a unique path to integration. Hartman is lightly linking the argument back to human capital discussion while examining the upward career mobility among the second generation Turks in Germany. He argues that the low labour market participation rates and educational attainment levels are undermining Turkish women's mobility chances and increases disadvantages over the life course. Sunata's paper is exploring the ways in which high skilled Turkish migrants deal with flexible working.

We hope this volume will offer new questions as well as answers to both academics and policy makers. Integration debates are increasingly more popular in Europe and patterns and outcomes related to Turkish migrant populations will be part of the agenda. Popularity of Turkish migration conferences and hundreds of academics apparently working on the subject are promising signs for a better understanding of population movements and repercussions in Europe and beyond.

Chapter 1: Union formation of Turkish migrant descendants in Western Europe: Family involvement in meeting a partner and marrying

Nadja Milewski and Doreen Huschek

One of the striking differences in family formation behaviour between Turkish and Western European cultures is in the role of family influence in the processes of partner choice and union formation. Family involvement has an impact on partner choice, as well as on other aspects of union formation, such as the type of union and the age at first union formation. Family involvement frequently occurs in Turkey and in other countries with a long Muslim tradition, and it remains important among emigrants and their descendants from these countries (de Valk & Liefbroer, 2007; Milewski & Hamel, 2010; Huschek et al., 2012; Baykara-Krumme, 2014; van Zantvliet et al., 2014; Topgül, 2015).

The differences in union formation practices in general and the role of the family in particular between Turkey and Western European countries have mainly been traced back to the overall differences between the respective family systems: one system has traditionally been characterised by collectivistic attitudes, intergenerational solidarity, and familial control; while the other system emphasises individualism and emotional closeness, and a lesser degree of intergenerational solidarity (Nauck & Suckow, 2002). In Turkey, family involvement in union formation, especially by the parents, is rationally motivated, and is seen as a function of intergenerational solidarity and intergenerational transmission (Sussmann, 1953; Straßburger, 2003). Hence, the partner choice is made not just by the two individuals, but also with the direct influence of the family. In individualistic societies, by contrast, union formation tends to be emotionally motivated, and the parents have no or little direct influence on their children's partner choice (Inglehart, 1997; Buunk et al., 2010).

Among emigrants, arranged marriages still make up a large share of the unions, but are less frequent than among non-migrants in Turkey (Baykara-Krumme, 2014). Previous research has also found variation by the country of origin of the migrants. However, the union formation patterns of Turks are found to be more similar to those of emigrants from Arabic countries than to the patterns among the Western European host populations (van Zantvliet et al., 2014). As the number of migrant descendants living in Western Europe grows, the question of how family behaviours are developing among members of the second generation is becoming increasingly important. On one hand, previous research on immigrants and their descendants in Western Europe has indicated that their family formation patterns are similar to those observed in Turkey; e.g., that the departure from the parental home, the first union, and the first marriage are strongly interrelated, and these events occur at relatively young ages (Hamel et al., 2012). On the other hand, compared to their parents, migrant descendants, and especially women, tend to have higher levels of education and labour force participation than their parents' generation (e.g, Crul et al., 2012). These factors are known to be associated with a weakening of intergenerational relations.

Our study adds to the literature by focusing on within-group variation among Turkish immigrant descendants living in seven Western European countries. We focus on different stages in the union formation process; i.e., how the partners met and whether the couple were discouraged or encouraged by family members in their decision to marry. In addition to looking at the individual's socio-demographic characteristics, we pay special attention to the role of the parental background and the relationship between the respondents and their parents.

Background and hypotheses

Family involvement in partner choice and union formation can take a variety of indirect forms, e.g. through social placing, and direct forms, which may not be clearly distinguishable from each other. For example, the potential partners may be casually introduced, or they may enter into an arranged union in which the partners first meet at their marriage ceremony. In extreme cases, they may be forced to marry. In some cases, the introduction of the potential partners may have been initiated by either set of parents, but the actual introduction is made by another family member, such as an older sibling. In cases in which the partners initiated their union/marriage themselves, they may seek the consent of their parents later on (Kagitçibasi & Ataca, 2005; Straßburger, 2003; Topgül, 2015). Sanctions may be a means of discouraging deviant behaviour (Kalmijn, 1998).

The literature ascribes several functions to family involvement. Parents may seek to maximise their social status and economic resources and may regard emotion as an insufficient basis for a stable union. The parents may therefore wish to ensure that the partners are a good match with regard to certain characteristics, such as religion, education, and age; as well as personality traits. It is assumed that if the partners are well matched, love will develop between them (Straßburger, 2003). Given the strong intergenerational ties in Turkish families, family involvement in partner choice is also a form of intergenerational transmission of values and norms. If these norms can be transmitted from one generation to the next, the potential for intergenerational conflicts is reduced, and family solidarity and social control is more likely to be preserved (Straßburger, 2003; Kagitçibasi & Ataca, 2005). Furthermore, parents generally prefer to have a son- or daughter-in-law who shares their language, values, and norms, as this will facilitate communication and cultural understanding between the families and promote social cohesion within the group (Kalmijn, 1998).

The process of partner choice and union formation leading to a marriage among Turkish migrants appears to be very similar to the process observed in Turkey. In general, the family of the potential husband plays the active part, though both partners have the agency to negotiate. Ideally, the process of partner selection follows five steps: 1) the search for a suitable bride, 2) visits between the respective families, 3) the marriage proposal and the decision to marry, 4) the marriage negotiations and ceremonies, and 5) the wedding (and, in cases of a transnational marriage, the marriage migration). Finally the couple moves into a joint household (Straßburger, 2003, Aybek et al., 2015; Topgül, 2015). Slight differences in this process may occur between migrant families and families living in Turkey because the spatial distance between Turkey and Western European countries, along with legal barriers to migration, can interfere with the steps of the partner selection process. Thus, modifications may be found in the spacing and the timing of the steps, but the overall process remains the same (Aybek et al., 2015).

However, in recent decades family involvement has declined somewhat in Turkey. As global urbanisation and modernisation trends have led to behavioural and societal changes in Turkey, new family values are developing among portions of the population. Today, the co-existence of two marriage regimes can be observed: affinal and descent. In the affinal marriage regime, conjugal solidarity, independent spouse selection, and romantic love are highlighted. In the descent regime, the emphasis is placed on the joining of families who wish to maximise their social status and economic resources, preserve family solidarity, and exert social control (Nauck & Klaus, 2008). In both forms, children and parents influence the partner choice to some degree, and most marriages are a hybrid form of the two marriage regimes. Parents may raise their children to be more autonomous in their life decisions, including partner choice, while at the same time demanding that the children uphold strong intergenerational family ties, and conform to the parents' preferences and expectations (Kagitçibasi & Ataca, 2005; Hortacsum, 2007). The modern family values are not spread equally among the population. They are most prominent among parents and children who have weak religious commitments, come from an urban area, have high levels of human capital, i.e., higher education, and have relatively small families (Kagitçibasi & Atacam, 2005; Hortacsum, 2007). Similar patterns have been found among Turkish migrants and their children (Celikaksoy et al., 2010; Milewski & Hamel, 2010; Muttarak, 2010; Munniksma et al., 2012). Higher levels of autonomy correspond to older than average ages at union formation (Bosma et al.,

14

1996). Hence, our first hypothesis relates to child autonomy; we expect to find that second-generation Turks with characteristics in line with a more autonomous upbringing will have experienced less family influence in their partner choice process.

Our second working hypothesis centres on the quality of the relationship between the child and his/her parents. Migrant families may be challenged due to differences in the acculturation process of parents and children. Families may search for a balance between retaining the norms, values, and behaviours of the culture of origin on one hand; and adopting some new behaviours relevant to the new socio-economic context on the other. If such an acculturation gap occurs, it is usually the children who have incorporated more of the values and behaviours prevalent in their current environment, while the parents are more likely to have maintained the values and behaviours of their country of origin (Kwak, 2003). Such an acculturation gap may strain the quality of the parent-child relationship. Families have fewer shared experiences, and misunderstandings and communication barriers may arise. These strained relations are often a source of conflict that threatens family cohesion (Qin, 2006; Renzaho et al., 2011). One possible cause of this acculturation gap is the proficiency in the language of the host country. When there is a large difference in the proficiency levels of parents and children, there can be a role reversal in the parent-child relationship, with the children having to take on more adult roles early in life. This may diffuse parental authority (Renzaho et al., 2011; Titzmann, 2012), and children may demand more autonomy in their decisions regarding their life choices, including their partner choice. We therefore expect to find that in cases in which there are many conflicts between the parents and the children, and the parents lack proficiency in the national language, the children will view any family involvement in their partner choice as unwanted, and will be less likely to experience parental involvement in their union formation.

Our third hypothesis takes into account the origin of the partner. According to Kalmijn (1994), the degree of cultural similarity is a trait that is much more predictable than, for example, economic factors, since the latter characteristics (such as occupation or income) vary much more over the life course. Following this logic, individuals should prioritise the cultural traits of their (future) spouse over other characteristics. We assume that parents want their children to select a partner from the same country of origin, since endogamous partner choice is a crucial means of maintaining social cohesion, facilitating communication within families, stabilising intergenerational relationships, and maintaining group identity and solidarity within a migrant community (Sussman, 1953; Kalmijn, 1998). Research has indicated that endogamy preference is transmitted from parents to their children in social contacts and dating behaviour during adolescence in Turkish communities (Nauck et al., 1997; Carol, 2014). Moreover, several studies have shown that "mixed" marriages—not only in terms of ethnicity or country of origin, but also with regard to education, religion, and various other social traits—have an elevated risk of dissolution, whereas endogamous Turkish couples have below-average divorce risks (Milewski & Kulu, 2014).

Data, variables, and method

Our sample comes from the survey The Integration of the European Second Generation (TIES 2007-08, Crul et al., 2012). The respondents were sampled as second-generation Turks if they were born in the country where the survey was held, at least one of their parents was born in Turkey, and they were 18 to 35 years old at the time of interview. An urban sample frame was used because most immigrants and their descendants throughout Europe live in cities. For all cities, a standardised questionnaire was used (Groenewold & Lessard-Phillips, 2012). Our study included Turkish second-generation youth from Amsterdam and Rotterdam in the Netherlands, Brussels and Antwerp in Belgium, Stockholm in Sweden, Paris and Strasbourg in France, Berlin and Frankfurt in Germany, Zurich and Basle in Switzerland, and Vienna and Linz in Austria. Our final sample consisted of 1,320 respondents (728 women, 592 men) who at the time of the interview were married or were cohabiting with a partner. In more than 90% of the cases, the current union was also the first union of the respondents.

Table 1.1 reports descriptive statistics for the variables used in our multivariate analyses as displayed in Table 1.2. We carried out logistic regression models with results reported as odds ratios. We used three dependent variables for family involvement in the union formation process. The first variable comes from a question about the way the respondents met their current partner. We grouped the answers (see Table 1.1) into a binary variable which captured direct family involvement versus all of the other ways in which the partners have met. The indicators of direct family involvement included responses that the partners met at a family celebration, through family network, or through an introduction by the parents. The response that the partners met during a holiday in Turkey appeared ambiguous, because the meeting may or may not have taken place within the family sphere. Hence, we included it in the "all other ways" category. The second and third dependent variables measured family involvement in the decision to marry (which usually appears at a later stage in the partner choice process, when a partner has already been chosen). The questions in the standardised questionnaire read "whether a respondent felt pressure from her/his family that encouraged (0 no, 1 yes) or discouraged (0 no, 1 yes) his/her marriage to his/her current partner." As the questions in the survey were phrased rather generally, we could not distinguish which family members encouraged the respondents to marry, and which discouraged them from marrying. We can only see whether the respondents felt that their family members were pressuring them in their partner choice and/or in their decision to marry.

Among the independent variables (see Table 1.1) used, one group contained characteristics of the respondents as well as their parents and their parental-child relationship. These were the respondents' education, whether they were raised according to a religion (if so, it was mainly a Muslim faith), whether respondents reported having had conflicts with their parents at age 17, the parents' proficiency

17

Table 1.1. Descriptive overview of the TIES sample

Dependent variables		%
Way of meeting[1]	Partner met within the family sphere (meeting at family celebration, through family network, introduced by parents)	23.7
	Partners met during holiday in Turkey	20.4
	Partners met outside the family sphere (school, university, work, through friends, at public place such as in the neighbourhood)	49.2
	Other/ Don't know	6.7
Family involvement in marriage decision[2]	Marriage discouraged	11.6
	Marriage encouraged	20.4
Independent variables		
Respondents' sex	Man	44.8
	Woman	55.2
Respondents' education	Special education/lower secondary	23.2
	Lower secondary & apprenticeship	30.6
	Upper-secondary & apprenticeship	28.3
	Tertiary education	17.9
Respondents' religious upbringing	No religious upbringing	14.6
	Raised according to a religion	32.5
	Attended Koran lesson/religious lessons outside school	52.9
Conflicts with parents at age 17 years	None	38.3
	Conflicts	21.5
	Missing/question not asked	40.2
Parents' language proficiency of country of residence	None	29.8
	One parent reads & writes in language of residence country	31.8
	Both parents read & write in language of residence country	38.4
Parents' origin (before age 15)	Both parents from rural area	40.2
	One parent from urban area	18.2
	Both parents from urban area	41.6
Respondents' age at union formation	14-19 years	20.6
	20-22 years	35.3
	23-25 years	25.4
	26+ years	18.7
Partners' origin[3]	First-generation partner from Turkey (G1)	51.0
	1.5-generation partner from Turkey (G1.5)	9.7
	Second-generation partner of Turkish descent (G2)	24.1
	Native partner from country of residence (N)	8.8
	Partner of other migrant origin or descent (O)	6.4
N		1320

Source: Calculations based on TIES 2007-08.
Note: [1] N=911 because the question on meeting place was not asked in Belgium and Sweden. [2] N=1320 in all seven countries. [3] G1=partner born in Turkey & came to Europe at age 17+; G1.5=partner born in Turkey, but migrated between ages 0 and 16 to Europe or attended school in Europe; G2=partner born outside Turkey to at least one Turkish parent; N=partner whose parents were born in one of the seven countries of the TIES survey; O=partner from another migrant group.

in the survey-country language, and the type of place where the respondents' parents grew up before age 15. The last set of variables referred to the union and the partner's origin.

Results

Way of meeting the partner

Table 1.1 shows that about 24% of the respondents met their partner within the family sphere and almost half (about 49%) of them met their partner outside the family sphere, such as through friends or at school (with little variation by sex). Another 20% of the respondents met their partner while on holiday in Turkey (which may be within or outside the family sphere). Regardless if the partners met through the family network or outside the family sphere, the majority (about 85%) of the partners were either first- or second-generation migrants from Turkey.

Table 1.2. Determinants of three types of family involvement in union formation (odds ratios)

Variables		M1 Direct family influence for meeting partner	M2 Discouraged in decision to marry	M3 Encouraged in decision to marry
Conflicts with parents at age 17 years	None	Ref	Ref	Ref
	Conflicts	0.92	2.42***	1.88**
	Missing/question not asked	1.54	0.87	0.81
Parents' language proficiency of country of residence	None	Ref	Ref	Ref
	One parent reads & writes in language of residence country	0.56**	0.81	0.90
	Both parents read & write in language of residence country	0.46***	0.52**	0.61*
Parents' origin (before age 15)	Both parents from rural area	Ref	Ref	Ref
	One parent from urban area	1.22	1.44	0.89
	Both parents from urban area	1.26	1.08	0.61**
Respondents' religious upbringing	No religiousupbringing	1.06	0.53*	0.80
	Raised according to a religion	Ref	Ref	Ref
	Attended Koran lesson/religious lessons outside school	1.48*	0.64*	1.27

Respondents' sex	Man	Ref	Ref	Ref
	Woman	0.88	1.73**	1.09
Respondents' education	Special education,/lower secondary	1.43	1.33	1.23
	Lower-secondary & apprenticeship	0.85	0.85	0.56*
	Upper-secondary & apprenticeship	Ref	Ref	Ref
	Tertiary education	0.65	0.91	0.79
	14-19 years	Ref	Ref	Ref
Respondents' age at union formation	20-22 years	0.69	0.95	0.69
	23-25 years	0.54*	1.07	0.57*
	26+ years	0.34***	0.76	0.55*
	First-generation partner from Turkey (G1)		Ref	Ref
	1.5-generation partner from Turkey (G1.5)		1.21	0.89
Partners' origin	Second-generation partner of Turkish descent (G2)		1.38	0.71
	Native partner from country of residence (N)		4.45***	0.76
	Partner of other migrant origin or descent (O)		4.25***	0.81
	N	911	1.32	1.32
	Log likelihood	-488.4	-430.9	-581.8
	Pseudo R²	0.102	0.0900	0.130

Source:Calculations based on TIES 2007-08.

Note: *** p<0.001, ** p<0.01, * p<0.05. Model 1 controlled for country of residence; Models 2 and 3 controlled for country of residence and type of union.

Model 1 (Table 1.2) explored which factors influenced the way in which the partners met. We investigated whether the partners met within the family sphere or in another way. The results show some support for our hypothesis regarding the quality of the parent-child relationship. Respondents who had one or two parents who were proficient in the language of the country of residence were less likely to have met their partner through the family than to have met the partner outside the family sphere. However, the number of conflicts with parents was not linked with having met the partner within the family sphere. When we look at the socio-demographic characteristics that are related to child autonomy, we found that the likelihood of having found a partner through the family network was higher the younger and the more religious the respondents were.

Encouraged or discouraged in the decision to marry

Finally, we studied whether the family influenced the respondent in his/her decision to marry his/her current partner (Table 1.2). In terms of discouragement (Model 2), we found that Turkish second-generation youth who reported any conflicts with their parents and those whose parents could not read and write in the language of the country of residence, were more likely to have been discouraged from marrying their current partner. The partner's origin also affected discouragement from marrying: Respondents with a non-migrant partner from the country of residence or a or a migrant partner from a third country were more likely to have reported that their parents discouraged their marriage than those with an endogamous partner choice. While having been discouraged from marrying was reported much more frequently by women than by men, other covariates were not found to have had a systematic and significant influence.

For encouragement to marry (Model 3), we found similar results concerning the quality of the intergenerational relationships. Respondents were more likely to have reported having been encouraged to marry if they were younger or older than average at the time of union formation, or if their parents were from a rural area. No systematic effect of education was found. This may be related to a correlation between this variable and the variables on age at union formation, religious upbringing, and origin of the parents. Overall, encouragement to marry was reported less frequently by respondents whose family of origin had characteristics associated with more individual autonomy.

Conclusion

In our paper, we studied family involvement in the partner choice and union formation processes among second-generation Turks living in Western European countries. Direct family involvement was reported in about one-quarter of the unions, which is in line with previous research on union formation in Turkey (Kagitcibasi & Ataca, 2005; Hortacsu, 2007; Nauck & Klaus, 2008). Family influence was more often reported in the introduction phase of the relationship, and was less often reported in the decision about whether to marry.

Concerning the determinants of family involvement, we found only partial support for our working hypothesis on child autonomy. Older respondents were more likely than younger couples to have initiated the meeting and made the decision about whether to marry. Education, religious upbringing, and the parents' place of origin were partially interrelated with this variable, and did not show clear systematic effects. We therefore conclude that the frequency and the patterns of family involvement no longer depend on these socio-demographic factors. Hence, couple-based partner selection has become common in Turkish migrant communities.

We found support for our hypothesis regarding the quality of the intergenerational relationships. A problematic parent - child relationship - whether due to conflicts in the teenage years or to an acculturation gap - was associated with the children having found their partner through the family network, and with the children feeling that their family pressured them in their marriage decision. Finally, we found evidence for an endogamy preference. If the partners were introduced by the family, then they were almost always of Turkish origin. Discouragement from marrying was most common if the partner was a non-migrant or a migrant from a third country. This finding is in accordance with previous research, which found that an endogamous partner choice is a means of maintaining social cohesion, facilitating communication, and stabilising intergenerational relation-ships (Sussman, 1953; Kalmijn, 1998).

Overall, couple-initiated unions are the major type of entering a union today. For the children of Turkish migrants Western Europe and Turkey are equally important marriage markets. If the family was involved in partner choice, then endogamous unions were supported, which suggests the maintenance of cultural norms and social cohesion within Turkish migrant communities. By adherence to the parents' norms and expectations, intergenerational ties, may be strengthened in turn.

Acknowledgement

Research by Nadja Milewski was supported by a European Reintegration Grant provided by Marie Curie Actions (FP7 People, PERG-GA-2009-249266 – MigFam) and funded by the European Commission. The views expressed in this paper do not reflect the views of the funding agencies.

Chapter 2: Turkish marriage ritual: Design for experience based embodied interaction

Johanna Kint and Sietske Klooster

Choreography of rituals in cultural context

Culture is becoming more complex, hidden in the small details of our intercultural society and in the subtleties of human behaviour. This complexity makes a first person perspective essential in order to gain a more thorough understanding of what culture, and cultural values are about. A first person perspective requires a more intuitive and sensorial exploration of culture, both for designers and for people to gain common knowledge on culture (Reed-Danahay, 1997).

The importance of rituals within this (re)search cannot be minimalized. General research has been developed by Bell on ritual theory and practice (Bell, 1992), by Rappaport on ritual and religion in the making of humanity (Rappaport, 1999) and many others. Van Gennep called them rites de passage. They mark forgiveness, reconciliation, or transitions to adulthood, married life, divorce, healing from sickness, and death (Van Gennep, 1977). In our globalizing world rituals still assert their significance by successfully negotiating structure and contingency, identity and hybridity, script and embodiment (Henn, 2008).

This research adds another layer and approach to this specific cultural context: choreography as embodied interaction based on experience (Wilde, 2011). We look for choreography and bodily interaction (Hummels, 2007) to touch upon the meaning of rituals within a small community from Emirdağ, Turkey, living in Brussels. Choreography brings us closer to the essence of what rituals are, and what they stand for within the context of this community, in relation to our society. We work by bodily interaction (Klooster, 2005) to get a better understanding of present-day marriage rituals, away from

25

prejudices. We develop new expressions through artefacts or objects that matter in this ritualized context. What is the relation between clothes or jewels, amongst others? What role do they play in the marriage ritual? How can we understand the relations by way of changing the objects or artefacts and the way they change the ritual?

Coming across the meaning of marriage rituals in the Turkish community

In Brussels the majority of immigrants with a Turkish background come from the region of Emirdağ (Teule, 2012). Theoretical research into the subject matter of marriage within Turkish communities in Belgium and emigration regions in Turkey has been developed at length (Timmerman, 2009). Our research revolves around creative and critical design practice, developed within this specific cultural context. We step out of theoretical framework and physically experience where the ritualized action is. We focus our attention on a different process, identified as reflection and action upon culturally embedded aesthetic and ethical values and their relevance to the language of dynamic form and gesture. Within the context of this process we look for different ways to enhance mutual respect and appreciation as a basic attitude to cultural dialogue and understanding.

Muslim lifecycle rituals - or rituals marking birth, circumcision, marriage, and death – are transposed and adapted to Western circumstances (Dessing, 2001). This research explores the possibilities of intercultural interaction and transformation through combined design and choreography. A novel ritual is created, inspired by a traditional Islamic-Turkish ritual, and interpreted in a Western European way. Bodily communication between and interaction with the two cultures is essential. Gulay K., living in the vicinity of Schaerbeek, kindly invited us to her house in Brussels. Together with her daughter, daughter-in-law and assisted by Cani N., she initiated us into the bodily expressions, dances and dress codes of the traditional Turkish marriage. She also invited us to the elaborate marriage festivities of her son and his future wife.

Although a modern and by Western standards very young couple (she was 21, he 24 when they married), bride and groom were very much committed to the traditional rituals of family and culture. During the marriage festivities the bride, for instance, was wearing vestigial gender symbols from the past, such as the red sash brides normally wear around their waist, confirming the idea that among Muslims, also in Turkey, marriage has always been considered the only legitimate form of cohabitation. According to Dessing, who in 2001 made an exhaustive research on rituals of birth, circumcision, marriage and death among Muslims living in the Netherlands, the basis for this can be found in the fundamentals of Islamic learning, according to which the aim of marriage is to legitimize sexual relations between partners. The family, which is based on marriage, forms the cornerstone of society. The family serves four main purposes, Dessing writes: 'It ensures reproduction, gives coherence to society, ensures the development of love and affection between husband and wife, as well as between parents and children, and provides a moral framework that regulates sexual relations and protects honour' (Dessing, 2001, p. 79).

Auto-ethnographic exploration of marriage rituals

The *Turkish Marriage Ritual* explores intercultural interaction and transformation through design and choreography. Sietske Klooster is a design - choreographer. The combination, moreover integration of design and choreography is her communication vehicle with other (sub) cultures. It is her way to discover a common ground and to consequently introduce novel shared rituals with inherent artefacts, which embody shared values. Klooster stands in-between the Muslim-Turkish community living in Schaerbeek, Brussels and her own Western European culture. She creates a novel ritual, 'cross-pollinating' the values behind traditional Turkish marriage ritual and our Western notion of it.

The marriage ritual is a complex issue. It is very confusing to understand from the perspective of our culture. *"I experience the Turkish marriage ritual"*, Sietske observes, *"as a process of transformation in family relations, more than a moment of bonding alone, such as our moment with exchanging rings. Choosing one particular Turkish ritual artefact was not an option from the beginning of the project. The Turkish marriage ritual is not built around one clear moment, point or object, but is a whole chain of events and places incorporating many accessories. I had planned to choose one object and investigate through that, but while working I discovered I could not do so, yet had to go through the maximum confusion about all things that happen. Though the basics are the same, I discovered also with the Turkish there are different ways of explaining the rituals and highlighting different elements of the values behind.”*

She continues: *“I therefore decided to first dive into this confusion, to bodily experience the process, instead of verbal interaction alone, to literally feel the basic experiential principle behind. Here I decided to let my own process of feeling an honest connection develop: where does it trigger a fundamental feel of common ground? Taking time to also let the feels of social cultural difference and even rejection happen, to sense where I felt an appealing ground for exchange.”*

“Not where we are the same, not where we are different, but where I feel space for exchange and mutual insights is the entrance to interact and share values. Such as combining the notion of equality between man and woman, with the notion of man and woman having different roles that complement each other to form a family that evolves.”

Why choosing the henna ritual after this explorative process? *“From the several ceremonies, the henna ritual or kina gecesi triggers recognition of an important moment in life that is not ritually supported by our culture: the moment of a woman, saying goodbye to her daughter-mother relationship, to make place for becoming a mother herself. This ritual in marriage focuses on the relating of families and the transformations in there. In this way the ritual does not only concern the marrying couple, but also family continuity. It also brings in the combination of saying goodbye and being welcomed at the same time; grief and joy as a combined emotion. Feasting this dichotomy of*

28

emotions feels as a very strong concept, which I recognize as a beautiful aspect of life, yet not so much celebrated in our culture."

Figure 2.1. Henna hand

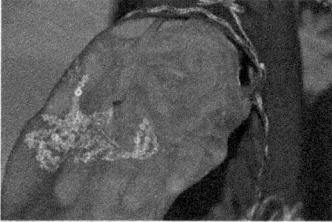

Figure 2.3. Film still

Figure 2.2. Film still

Source: Moving Rituals (movie) (2013)

Designing choreographic exploration of marriage rituals

Sietske Klooster's interpretation of the henna ritual focuses on the combination of letting go and bonding, integrated in one object or artefact that supports both. She designed a sleeve that is worn from the wrist, covering the hand(s). The sleeve is the carrier of two transition moments: on the one hand the untangling and literal loosening moment of letting go of the mother-daughter relationship; on the other hand the intertwining moment of alliance with a man to start a new family. In its loosened state and after letting go with the mother, the sleeve holds the state of being on ones own until the right partner is found to start a new family. In its entangled state it is kept to remember the bonding with the husband, till the moment comes when the woman has to let go of her own daughter when she's grown up and will move into independence.

To develop her interpretation of the henna ritual, Klooster explored the role of hand palm, as this body part is central in the Turkish Muslim ritual (Figure 2.1). The reason for henna application on this body part is not univocal and involves a myriad of practical and symbolic levels. Yet instead of rationally determining the pragmatic and symbolic origin of this body part, Klooster decided to experience her interpretation of movement pivoting around the palm of the hand, both in the act of separation (mother-daughter) and in the bonding (husband-wife) (Figure 2.2). She primarily searched for the meaning experienced through the movement, since movement provides a common understanding or, as Schwartz mentions within the context of the relationship between the dancer or performer and his/her stage, 'the body must be realized as a matrix of meaning. We learn to think from the body outward' (Schwartz, 1996, p.79). Because of this matrix, people who speak different languages may often be able to communicate with the language of gesture. Schwartz: 'Everyone shares a common repertoire of action schemes, even though there are instances in which specific gestures convey different or even opposite meanings in different cultures' (Schwartz, 1996, p.81).

The 'hand palm' feel is essential in the feelings of contact and bonding. As a result Sietske's ritual consequently pivots around the palms of the hands, as it is in the henna ritual. Just like with the henna ritual, the sleeve forms a rose-shape in the palm of the hand, when entangled. In the untangled shape the hand palm is free and open for a novel relation. This is the contemporary intermediate Western European state that developed over the last decades. The woman can keep this free status until she feels stable and flexibly independent. She can choose the moment to start a new bonding process or the bonding of a woman and a man in an act of symmetry and mutuality.

A novel cross-cultural symbolism is initiated here through bodily investigation and physical interaction with Turkish community members. When making a novel artefact, Klooster mentioned, there is the danger of becoming enticed by known symbolism and of the object as such. Klooster specifically tried to feel the delicate difference between the object as carrier of symbolism and the factual experience of a ritual movement and its inherent meaning, facilitated by a ritual object. By material retrenchment and embodied investigation, as can be seen in Figure 2.3, the designer escapes the existing 'frozen' symbolism and finds what lies underneath it and felt in the physical experience of the ritual movement. From this bodily basis it is possible to investigate the experience of value exchange, or at least values that are mutually understood. This is where contemporary living and thus dynamic symbolism and tradition can arise, in close connection with a mutual embodied understanding of ritual meaning and values between cultures.

Epilogue or lessons to be learned

First of all, we would not have been able to develop this research without the hospitality of a Turkish Islamic family, living in Schaerbeek, Brussels. We have been invited on several occasions at the house of a Turkish woman and her large family, with coffee, tea and sweets. This lady also kindly invited us as her guests at the wedding rituals of her son, and his future wife. This unstrained and warm hospitality from a family that in the sixties migrated from Emirdağ, Turkey, to Belgium struck us as a quality that since the sixties is fading away in our hyper-individualistic and xenophobic Western society.

Secondly, the entire creative process of approaching the marriage ritual through choreography and designed artefact, as developed by Sietske Klooster, has closely been followed by two audio-visual students and captured in a movie. After completion, we showed this movie to a female student from a Turkish migration family who also attends an audio-visual training at our university college. She was surprised by the fact that we were interested in the marriage ritual of her culture and that we researched this issue. She watched the movie and concluded our research to be much more relevant than she initially would have imagined. At first she thought our research to be an –

obvious - interpretation of a ritual she is confronted with weekly: nearly every weekend, she told us, she is invited to a marriage party (as we would say in the West) somewhere in her hometown and surroundings. The marriage ritual has become evidence within her daily life activities. She was much surprised by our careful and close observation and lecture of the henna ritual, scrutinizing beauty and inner meaning through careful gestures and movements, which initially caught our attention and afterwards, by viewing our movie, also caught hers. It made her perceive the richness of her culture and its rituals in a different way, and made her aware of the importance of its hidden meaning from and for a Western perspective. It also made her sensitive on how, by changing perception and approach, one opens up to dialogue and mutual understanding. This is what in essence the meaning of art, and design is. And hers was the most daring compliment, besides the warm congratulations we received after presenting our movie at the 2014 Turkish Migration Conference in London.

Thirdly. We estimate that the *Turkish Marriage Ritual* might introduce a novel approach and level to cultural studies: creative bodily interaction as a way to explore common ground and value exchange. We work by body language and creative interaction, instead of cognitive analysis of differences alone (Kint, 2010). Through creative bodily interaction, in an active social intercultural context, we perform and develop meaning, which enables us to bring about value exchange and cultural transformation in a poetic way.

Last but not least, we do not think the *Turkish Marriage Ritual* to be a finished story. It is meant as a starter for further interaction and intercultural communication. We intend to further reflect on this first part of the project with a Turkish Muslim family in the company of a Western European family. This we plan to do as a bridge to a second trajectory, where a designer with roots in Turkish Muslim culture takes over the current design and choreography of Klooster and through the act of co-designing with her and a Western family, brings about a next iteration, manifesting his or her embodied explorations and interpretations. Thus design and choreography eventually might become a new language for intercultural exchange and interaction, besides mutual understanding of different rituals.

Chapter 3: Rethinking loyalty (vefa) through transnational care practices of older Turkish women in Sweden

Öncel Naldemirci

First-generation Turkish immigrants in Sweden have started to reach older ages and to think about their old age and future care needs. Strong family and community ties, intergenerational solidarity, and cultural practices regulating marriage, socialization and care are believed to be a characteristic of Turkish families (Liljeström & Özdalga, 2002). However, as Finch and Mason argue, *"responsibilities between kin are not straightforward products of rules of obligation, they are (...) the products of negotiation"* (1993, p. 60). An increasing number of studies attempt to understand how families are made and remade in the migration context through care relations, responsibilities and negotiations (Baldassar, 2001, 2007, 2008; Bryceson & Vuorela, 2002). In this paper, I will highlight the role of emotions in negotiating and thinking about care responsibilities in a migration context and argue that emotions not only redefine transnational care practices but they also reshape the ways in which family responsibilities are imagined in diaspora space (Brah, 1996). After briefly describing the methods of the research, focus will be directed towards exploring the significance of emotions in migration studies. Then I will focus on a particular emotion – *vefa* – and discuss how it is translated into gendered care practices, by referring to three older Turkish women's accounts.

Method

This paper draws upon three older Turkish women's life stories and accounts about their gendered and intergenerational care experiences and practices. These stories and accounts were selected from a larger ethnographic study that consisted of observations and semi-structured in-depth interviews with 20 Turkish participants, 10 women, and 10 men, who lived in a former industrial city situated on the west coast of Sweden between 2011 and 2013. All of my informants were over 60, with a considerable variation in age range. The women were generally younger than the men, most of whom were over 70. All of the informants in this study immigrated to Sweden during the late 1960s and early 1970s. They were retired and naturalized Swedish citizens, and they had chronic illnesses and were familiar with medical institutions in Sweden. I used a narrative approach (Ricoeur, 1984) to analyse the transcribed material and field notes by focusing on "narrative environments" (Gubrium & Holstein, 2009).

Emotionalization of family

Skrbiš (2008) identifies five major areas of research concerning emotions and transnational families: emotional labour as a dimension of transnational family life, emotion and the experience of co-presence, emotions and longing, emotionalizing the national family, and emotional expressions in migrants' writings. The list is not exhaustive, but it underlines the major preoccupations in the field. The aim here is to contribute to the literature concerning emotionalization of family, by arguing that the set of emotions which Turkish elderly people deploy paves the way for a particular way of negotiating family responsibilities, ethnic identification, and different ideals of care. These emotions work to align the individual with the collective (Ahmed, 2004) and serve to create an ideal family environment where the first-generation Turkish immigrants and their offspring are positioned in between a Swedish family, which is imagined to be modern but uncaring, and a Turkish family, which is perceived to be traditional, demanding and oppressive. Deploying emotions leads to making Turkish family by constantly imagining it in relation to the Swedish society. As Bryceson and Vuorela argue, "the inclusion of dispersed members within the family is confirmed and renewed through various exchanges and *points of contact*. (2002, p. 10, *emphasis added*).

A particular set of emotions like *merhamet*, *şefkat*, and *vefa* (Naldemirci, 2013) are meant to create new points of contact for the older Turkish migrants, to give meaning to their identity, difference, and sense of continuity. When an older parent emphasizes how his children are loyal to the family, not only does he embrace a well-praised ideal of the Turkish family but also transmutes his desire (to be a respected father) and fear (of not being so) to his life in Sweden. The Turkish family to which older migrants refer is not a monolithic institution, detached from the experience of being an immigrant in Sweden. Instead, it becomes a way of expressing their individual life stories by linking these to a diasporic repertoire of 'Turkishness'. This repertoire does not derive from an unchanging Turkishness, it is anchored in a continuous imagination and negotiation of 'Swedishness' and 'Turkishness' in diaspora space through emotions.

Emotions in diaspora space

Migration overwhelmingly changes the context of social relations, and as Ian Burkitt argues, *"emotions have meaning only in the context of relations, involving active bodily states or feelings and the speech genres through which we attempt to articulate those feelings"* (2002, p. 153). Migration brings about changes in how people understand and express their emotions. Not only do immigrants notice that their ways of expressing and feeling emotions are entrenched in their cultural identity, but they also interpret emotional scripts that they encounter in the host country. Transnational relations and flows of information, stories, and experiences lead to changing meanings of taken-for-granted emotions.

An increasing amount of research on transnationalism and migration has started to take emotions into consideration as a relevant source of information about identities and cultures (cf. Skrbiš and Svašek, 2007; Gray, 2008; Skrbiš, 2008, Svašek 2010). As Skrbiš and Svašek argue, "mobile individuals are tied to their families and friends 'back home,' but they also grow attachments to their new surroundings, learn to express feelings in new ways, and have particular hopes and expectations about what the future may bring" (2007, p. 373). The new surroundings, objects, ways of doing in the host country as well as memories and information from the country of departure pave the way for a particular imagination, and diverse ways of feeling the world. In other words, in order to grasp what identities are sought and performed in transnational and/or diasporic communities, and what meanings circulate, it is crucial to come to grips with emotions. Emotions involve both meaning and feeling (Leavitt, 1996) in the sense that human beings not only feel bodily emotions but also make sense of specific social contexts through emotions.

Diasporic communities are also conjured up and maintained through a special affective economy. According to Sara Ahmed, "emotions define the contours of the multiple worlds that are inhabited by different subjects" (2004, p. 25) and "emotions do things, and work to align individuals with collectives" (2004, p. 26). Emotions shape the boundaries of the collective. What, for, and with whom emotions will be felt not only defines the boundaries of diasporic community but also generates an active emotionalization of families, friendship, and relations with community members. Emotions not only mark the boundaries of a diasporic community but also shape subject positions for members in the community. The native, the other, or the hegemonic come to be represented as being devoid of these emotions.

The experience of migration catalyzes a wide range of affects and emotions. From loneliness to solidarity, from nostalgia to homing, a variety of emotions are felt and assessed among diasporic subjects, and this lies at the core of imagination and/or building a sense of belonging and community. Therefore, studying emotions can help us to challenge the essentialist and culturist ways of defining diaspora. For instance, loyalty to the (real or imagined) homeland is a well-known emotion in diasporic and transnational communities. Loyalty is experienced and demonstrated via a wide range of transnational practices, such as regular visits, sending remittances, and maintaining transnational family and kinship ties. However, loyalty can also gain strength in diaspora space and come to define a Turkish family and a caring diasporic community. These processes cannot be properly understood without the analysis of the emotions they accompany.

Vefa

Vefa is a protean and polysemic emotion and means loyalty, fidelity, faithfulness and consistency in love in common usage in the Turkish language. Someone who feels *vefa* remembers the good old days, where one was genuinely loved, respected, and cared about. *Vefa* is therefore a question of memory and is rooted in the reminiscence of past emotional, financial, and practical help. It articulates the goodness and trust received in the past, and projects the hope for help and care in the future. It creates a dyadic relationship and a readiness to reciprocate. However, it does not impose any direct and immediate return of past kindness. It is anchored in a particular gift economy (Godbout, 1998) and a sense of connectivity (Joseph, 1993). *Vefa* can be deeply felt but it can be expressed at irregular intervals. For instance, visits to the country of origin, regardless of their motives and frequency, show that migrants did not renounce their roots, friends, and family members left behind. A disloyal (*vefasız*) migrant is expected to compensate for her past mistakes and absences.

Even though *vefa* is a familiar trope in Turkey, it is worth noting that it gains greater emphasis in the migration context as an emotional response to the anxiety, guilt, and shame of emigration (cf. Chamberlain and Leydersdof, 2004). Remittances, gifts, regular phone calls, being careful not to miss significant family events, such as weddings and funerals are significant ways to demonstrate *vefa*. Loretta Baldassar's work (2001, 2007) underlines emotional dimensions of long-distance relationships between parents left in Italy and their children who emigrated to Australia. She explores different patterns of "staying in touch" and argues that migrants and their families engage with not only practical and financial support, but also emotional support. I also noticed similar practices of providing economic, practical and emotional support to older parents and kin who stayed in Turkey. Being and staying loyal to family and friends in the homeland was a recurrent theme. As a double-edged emotion, *vefa* defines the good Turkish migrant who did not forget her native country, nor friends and family in that home country, while it also offers a significant way

39

of making Turkish family in the diaspora space. *Vefa* refers to a family history shaped by the experience of migration and transnational relations. It is anchored in the moral economy of people who are engaged in a gift economy, not only with people they left in their native country, but also in the country of settlement.

There are gendered ways of feeling loyal and being consistent in love. Not only do emotions have "ascribed meaning that tends to be gender-specific" (Peterson, 2005), but the same emotions are also embodied, experienced, and demonstrated differently. The feeling of culpability (Baldassar, 2008) is balanced with gendered practices and expressions of *vefa*. While men can remain loyal to their families by giving practical and financial support, even across borders, in other words, by "taking care of" their family members, whereas women feel more to "care for" and "care about" their family members who did not emigrate (for different components of care, see Tronto, 1993). In what follows, I will illustrate the gendered repercussions of this protean emotion.

Melahat

Melahat had been a tailor in a big city in Turkey. In 1969, she married a pioneer migrant who had settled in Sweden. She moved first to a small city in Sweden, where she started to work in a textile factory. Even though she did not like the city, which was very different from her native city across the Aegean Sea, she was not completely displeased with her new job. The factory environment was nothing like the tailor shop where she used to work, but at least she was still dealing with fabrics and threads. A year later, she and her husband moved to a larger city, and Melahat started to work in the automobile industry. There the work was strenuous. As she did not have a happy marriage, she deeply regretted her emigration. Melahat, after her divorce, brought her older mother to Sweden, and she cared for her in order to compensate for the years they had lived apart.

> *I lived my best years with my mother. I felt as if I left her alone, as if I were an ungrateful (vefasız) offspring when I got married*

and migrated to Sweden. I was the only daughter in the family. Of course I was traveling back to Turkey but it was great when my mother came here. We caught up the years we lost. I could care for her here when she was unwell. She passed away here. I really miss her but I don't have any regrets anymore.

Melahat's feeling of guilt after emigration was caused by her not being able to care about and for her mother as she had wished. When her mother joined her in Sweden, she was eager to engage in hands on care and felt less guilty. In other words, she got the chance to demonstrate her loyalty to her mother before it was too late.

Selma

Selma was in her early sixties at the time of the interview and she had already engaged in many transnational care visits. When she came to Sweden in the 1960s, like Melahat, she felt guilty in the first years after she emigrated. She tried to stay in touch with her family first by sending letters and visits once a year, then regular phone calls. She travelled back to Turkey in order to take care of her family members, first her older brother, then her mother. Unlike Melahat's mother, Selma's mother had three daughters. For Selma, care in old age was a family responsibility, both a question of compassion towards the elderly and a way to demonstrate loyalty to the family. She was not expected to travel to Turkey when her mother was unwell and needed care; Selma's sister was already there to take care of their mother. Nevertheless, Selma immediately went to Turkey to show her that even though she was geographically away, she was emotionally attached to her and ready to care for her. During her stay, she provided hands-on care for her mother; this caring practice was a way to express loyalty and love to her mother. Selma described her motivation to travel to Turkey as:

My sister was there. They did not really need me, my mother had already been hospitalized and I was a perfect stranger in this Turkish hospital anyways. I could not stay here [Sweden]. I wanted to show my mother that I had been and was her loyal [vefalı] daughter. After so many years away from them, I felt I had to be there. Fortunately, I was there since my mother passed away a month later [after I arrived].

Memnune

Memnune was another early-in-life immigrant who joined her husband in Sweden. Just after her arrival to Sweden, she had to combine her caring responsibilities with menial work. She was the mother of five children and was exhausted both at work and at home. First, she left her children at day care, but it still proved to be difficult with all the arrangements. They lived away from a day care centre. Memnune and her husband worked different shifts, and he used to help with collecting the children from day care; Memnune dealt with the rest. At the end she was completely weary and had to find a solution. First, they left small children in Turkey with their grandmother, then, Memnune's mother moved to Sweden to take care of them until they were older; she stayed six years and then went back to Turkey.

May God rest her soul, my loyal [vefakar], my beautiful mother. If she had not come, I would not have survived. I really don't know what we would have done if my mother had not come to care for the children. She left everything and came here to take care of children.

These three different stories of caregiving and receiving illustrate how care practices are anchored in the making of a transnational family. Not only are these practices motivated by strong feelings and commitments, but they are also deeply rooted in a particular imagination of the family through gendered practices of elderly and child care.

Vefa in diaspora space

Vefa is also relevant in making Turkish family within diaspora space. The assumption and stereotypical view of the Swedish family is that family members invest emotionally in their children until they are adults, whereas as the migrants they saw themselves more engaged in mutual support and reciprocity in the family in order to overcome the difficulties of being in a foreign land *(gurbet)*. Memnune put it this way:

> *Memnune: We are very different from the Swedish families. When the Swedish are 18 years old, the family disintegrates. When one is 18 years old, he or she leaves the [family] home. Even if the child does not want to, parents encourage him or her to leave, to live with friends or partners. But we think that children should stay until they get married. We don't stop caring about them, in one way or another. They stop caring about their children when they are 18.*

> *Interviewer: So, you mean that Turkish children continue to care about their parents?*

> *Memnune: They keep caring about us too.*

> *Interviewer: How do you think they are attached to parents?*

> *Mennune: I think it is due to love they have seen in/from us, but I have never constricted my children. There are some very authoritative [Turkish] families, they say: "Where are you going my son?" "Don't go there" "Don't have a girlfriend." They oppress their children. I haven't.*

Memnune refers to the Turkish family as a caring environment where children are loved and therefore they are inclined to show love to their parents in return. She positions the ideal Turkish family in between the carefree, less emotional Swedish family and the oppressive and backward Turkish family. A caring parent-child relationship is idealized and imagined to shape the children into a caring subjectivity. Therefore, *vefa*, as consistency in love, places the family responsibilities and caring relations into a family history. The shared family history gains primordial importance in future family relations and decision making. It refers to a common repertoire of norms (caring parents and loyal children who are consistent in their love) without neglecting the variability of practices and experiences depending on individual family histories. By calling their adult children loyal, they

43

invited them to return certain services and created a proper subject position for both themselves and their children as Turkish people. When the filial duty is understood on the basis of *vefa*, the intergenerational solidarity comes to be rooted in a caring environment.

Emotionalizing family through *vefa* leads to two main understandings. First, family invokes once again the "good old days," when parents offered a new life to their children in a foreign country despite all of the difficulties involved, and now it is the adult children's turn to reciprocate in caring relations. *Vefa* appears to be a claim to authenticity by maintaining the possibility of being independent and autonomous individuals. Loyalty to the family wishfully invites adult children to assume their responsibilities for their elderly by pointing to their difference, as Turkish, from the rest of the society. Selma's spouse Adnan, after a long account of how busy his son was, said:

Our children are loyal [vefalı] [to us, the elderly of the family]. They are born and raised here [in Sweden]. But they are like that, they would not feel comfortable letting us down.

Second, deploying *vefa* as a particular emotional discourse challenges the filial responsibilities and obligations that are considered to be traditional, backward, or at least too demanding. *Vefa* paves the way for demanding more than might be deemed reasonable in the Swedish context. Even if they fail to provide hands-on care, by being *vefalı*, loyal to their elderly, the adult children can continue to care about their parents, and mark their difference from others who are not caring about elderly at all. As Selma put it:

Even if they [children] put me in an elderly home, I know that that they wouldn't forget me there. They would visit me more often than others' children do.

One can demonstrate *vefa* by visiting parents in an elderly home, while another may voluntarily offer home help; but still being loyal to their shared past as family, they do not lose their identity as Turkish people. This rather becomes an understandable and modern way of shaping and appropriating family responsibilities through emotions.

Conclusion

The emotionalization of the family is one underlying discourse in diaspora communities (Skrbiš, 2008, p. 240) and this inevitably affects how older immigrants perceive their older ages, care needs, and family relations. The concept of love for the young and respect for the elderly (*sevgi ve saygı*) has long been the *leitmotiv* of the ideal Turkish family, and this has contributed to the definition of roles in the family based on a hierarchical interdependence (cf. Liljeström and Özdalga, 2002). Here I argue that we also need to take more protean emotions into account, in order to better understand ruptures and continuities in care responsibilities in a migration context. Rather than putatively locating negotiations and responsibilities in family and close kinship, we need an analysis of emotions, which ascribe particular caring practices to particular gendered and moral positions. *Vefa* as a protean and polysemic emotion not only defines and motivates transnational care practices, but it also shapes expectations and understandings of care in diaspora.

Chapter 4: Who takes part in a cross sectional survey on health care service utilisation among Turkish and German nationals in Germany? [1]

Ulrike Zier and Stephan Letzel

Socio-cultural aspects of health such as understanding of sickness and health, or symptom awareness are likely to influence health care utilisation as well as system knowledge or financial and communicational obstacles to health care access. In a multicultural society like Germany, health care services and policy regulation have to take this issue into account, in order to provide equal access. The share of inhabitants with foreign nationalities has risen from 1.2% (0.7 million) in 1961 to 9.5% (7.6 million) in 2013[2] (Statistisches Bundesamt, 2014a, p. 27-37). Most foreign nationals in Germany are Turkish citizens. They make up a share of 20.3% of all foreign nationals and 1.9% of all inhabitants. Even though health care utilisation is an important means of maintaining and restoring personal health, the question of whether different socio-cultural patterns exist has not been addressed comprehensively by previous research in Germany. Only a few studies on specific aspects of the topic exist and mention barriers in health care access (e.g. Bermejo, Hölzel, Kriston, & Härter, 2012; Robert Koch Institut, 2008). With our survey we cover a broad range of research questions on general health care utilisation practices in a representative population sample of Turkish and German nationals.

Our survey is, like others, restricted in its representativeness by selective participation. Low participation has to be expected especially for Turkish nationals, since migrants in general are regarded as a

---

[1] Findings presented in the paper will be part of the thesis of Ulrike Zier.
[2] Due to different data bases, next to reported number based on the Central Register of Foreigners there is another number of foreign nationals reported of 6.9 million persons based on the Current Population Estimation.

population hard to reach and unfamiliar with written surveys (Kohler, Rieck, Borch, & Ziese, 2005; Schenk & Neuhauser, 2005). Furthermore there is evidence that individuals with lower social status and those living alone are less likely to participate in surveys. However, there are contradictory reports on the effect of sex, age, urbanity of the place of residence and health status (Blohm & Diehl, 2001; Kohler et al., 2005; Schenk & Neuhauser, 2005).

Whereas our study aims to better understand health care utilisation of German und Turkish nationals, here, we present results on the representativeness of the sample realized. In order to get insights into participatiory behaviour in these population groups we analysed possible associations of socio-demographic and health-care related variables with participation.

Method

We conducted a cross sectional written survey in the federal state of Rhineland-Palatinate. Study design and materials were approved by the data protection commissioner of Rhineland-Palatinate and the ethical review committee of the state board of physicians of Rhineland Palatinate. We decided to conduct the survey in Rhineland-Palatinate, since contact data for the target population could be obtained on federal state level. Due to the objective of a preferably homogenous population in respect to health-care need, we aimed to reach individuals of working age. Therefore, the target population of the survey were registered with primary residence in the federal state, aged 20 to 65 years and had Turkish or German citizenship.

To make sure we get sufficient information on Turkish immigrants, we decided to stratify our sample by nationality and thereby oversample Turkish nationals. After additional permission from the Ministry of the Interior of Rhineland-Palatinate, a sample of 4,000 addresses of persons in the target group was drawn from all local registry offices in the federal state. The sample was stratified by nationality, meaning one stratum of 2,000 addresses contained information on persons with Turkish or Turkish and German nationality and another stratum of 2,000 that of persons with German nationality only (see Fig. 1). Both strata were drawn by simple random sampling. Data was acquired via KommWis - Gesellschaft für Kommunikation und Wissenstransfer mbH[3] and delivered on May 15th 2013. Together with names, addresses and nationality we were provided with registration offices' data on sex, date of birth, marital status and the first 6 digits of the official community code of the sampled persons. According to the Regional Bureau of Statistics there were 45,424 persons in the age group 20 to 65 years with Turkish citizenship in Rhineland-Palatinate in 2013 and 2,249,598 persons with German nationality (Statistisches Bundesamt, 2014b). Our sample consists of about 4% of the target population in the first stratum and of about 0.1% in the second stratum.[4]

We sent envelopes with an information letter, questionnaire, declaration of non-participation as well as a stamped and self-addressed envelope to all addresses on June 12th 2013. Whereas for the German stratum all study materials were provided in German language only, for the Turkish stratum they were provided in Turkish additionally. A native speaker translated all documents and qualitative testing took place with four German and Turkish nationals each. An ID was assigned to each address and printed on study material. The declaration of non-participation contained questions on self-rated health (how is your state of health in general: very good/ good/moderate/bad/very bad), health care satisfaction (how satisfied are you with healthcare in

---

[3] The company is affiliated to the Association of Towns and Municipalities of Rhineland-Palatinate, the Cities Council of Rhineland Palatinate and the County Association of Rhineland-Palatinate.

[4] In the depiction persons with the German and an additional citizenship are considered German citizens. According to the Microcensus about 1.9% of the German citizens within the age group have dual citizenship (Statistisches Bundesamt (2013), p. 123-132) and are therewith not part of the target group for the second stratum. Out of those German nationals with dual citizenship in the age group 33.2% have a citizenship of a European country which is no member state of the European Union. Assuming generously that dual citizenships with one being the Turkish citizenship make up for half of them, the target group for the first stratum would rise by 16.6%. Following these estimations the first stratum would consist of 3.9% and the second of 0.1% of the target population.

Germany: very satisfied/ satisfied/ moderate/ unsatisfied/very unsatisfied) and number of visits to the doctor (how often have you visited a doctor in Germany in the last 12 months) to be answered voluntarily. Those questions were also asked in the questionnaire. Reaction to the questionnaire (returned to sender, filled questionnaire, declaration of non-participation, no reaction) was marked in the address-dataset, which was stored separately. Until August 2013 up to two reminders were sent to those who did not react before.

Figure 4.1. Process of data collection and reactions of the sampled persons

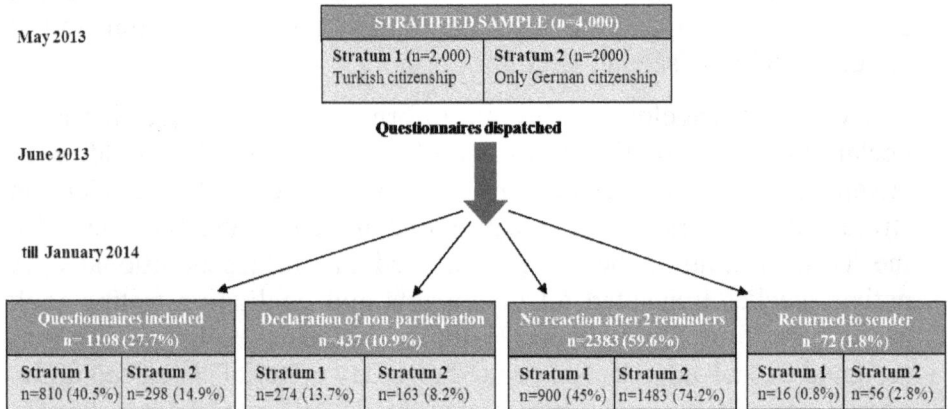

In August all names and addresses were deleted and an anonymized dataset was exported containing ID, participation, nationality, sex, age on June 12th 2014, marital status, and urbanity of the community (Statistische Ämter des Bundes und der Länder, 2014). We converted questionnaires and declarations of non-participation into electronic format using a document scanner with forms processing software and matched datasets by ID. To contrast the deliberate decision to participate or not to, we excluded data of persons that could not be reached. Furthermore, questionnaires filled by other than the target person[5] were treated as no reaction.

An error probability of $\alpha = 0.05$ was assumed for all statistical tests. Absolute and relative frequencies were calculated for socio-demographic and health care related variables. Bivariate associations between those variables and reaction to the questionnaire were analysed by means of chi-square test. For multivariate analysis we created a dichotomous variable: participation - yes/no. 'No' contained cases with no reaction and those who sent back a declaration of non-participation. In order to estimate independent effects of the socio-demographic and health care variables on participation, binary logistic regression models (inclusion method) were calculated for both strata and the whole sample. Cases with missing values were excluded from bivariate and multivariate testing.

Results

The age of the sampled persons was distributed around a mean age of 38.9 years in the Turkish and 44.2 years in the German stratum. The share of females was 48.5% and 51.2% respectively in the two strata. Comparing them with the population statistics (Statistisches Bundesamt, 2014b), both strata are representative for the target groups regarding the distribution of age and sex.

We excluded 17 questionnaires as not filled by the target person. The overall response rate considering only questionnaires that were delivered (n=3,928) was 27.7%. Turkish nationals were considerably less likely to take part (14.9% vs. 40.5%) (See Fig. 4.1).

Bivariate analyses show that in both strata, singles were significantly less likely to react to the questionnaire at all and to fill out the questionnaire. In the German stratum the same was true for men and younger persons. Considering only those who reacted by means

---

[5] Questionnaires were excluded if either own statements on sex differed from registry data and age differed more than one year or if only age differed more than ten years.

Table 4.1. Prevalences for socio-demographic and health variables stratified by participation and p-values for chi-quare text (missing values excluded)

VARIABLE		TURKISH STRATUM							GERMAN STRATUM						
		p	Questionnaire n=298	%	Refusal n=163	%	No reaction n=1483	%	p	Questionnaire n=810	%	Refusal n=274	%	No reaction n=900	%
Sex	Female	p=0.190	145	15.4	87	9.2	702	74.5	p<0.001	455	44.8	167	16.4	394	38.8
	Male		153	15.3	76	7.6	781	77.9		355	36.7	107	11.1	506	52.3
Age	20-35	p=0.066	102	12.8	62	7.8	635	79.5	p<0.001	167	30.2	57	10.3	329	59.5
	36-45		96	16.2	54	9.1	444	74.7		155	36.7	72	17.1	195	46.2
	46-55		72	19.6	28	7.6	267	72.8		258	44.6	82	14.2	238	41.2
	56-65		28	15.2	19	10.3	137	74.5		230	53.4	63	14.6	138	32.0
Marital status	Married	p=0.021	225	16.1	129	9.2	1047	74.7	p<0.001	551	45.7	181	15.0	473	39.3
	Single		46	12.4	17	4.6	308	83.0		181	31.8	63	11.1	325	57.1
	Divorced/Widowed		26	15.5	16	9.5	126	75.0		78	37.1	30	14.3	102	48.6
	Not stated		1	25.0	1	25.0	2	50.0		0	0.0	0	0.0	0	0.0
Urbanity	Urban	p=0.357	99	14.8	52	7.8	518	77.4	p=0.711	128	38.0	44	13.1	165	49.0
	Semi-urban		164	14.9	95	8.6	843	76.5		381	41.4	129	14.0	411	44.6
	Rural		35	20.2	16	9.2	122	70.5		301	41.5	101	13.9	324	44.6
Self-rated health	(Very) Good	p=0.038	152	69.1	68	30.9			p=0.399	563	84.0	107	16.0		
	Moderate/(Very) Bad		134	78.8	36	21.2				239	81.8	53	18.2		
	Not stated		12	16.9	59	83.1				8	6.6	114	93.4		
Satisfaction with health care	(Very) Satisfied	p=0.871	151	71.9	59	28.1			p=0.021	527	77.7	151	22.3		
	Moderate/(Very)Unsatisfied		138	72.6	52	27.4				268	66.0	138	34.0		
	Not stated		9	14.8	52	85.2				15	12.3	107	87.7		
Number of visits to the doctor	0-6	p<0.001	144	67.3	70	32.7			p<0.001	400	78.1	112	21.9		
	7 to 12		76	84.4	14	15.6				233	87.3	34	12.7		
	>12		67	89.3	8	10.7				175	95.1	9	4.9		
	Not stated		11	13.4	71	86.6				2	1.7	119	98.3		

of sending back a questionnaire or a declaration of non-participation, a significantly increased participation rate can be seen for those visiting the doctor more often in both strata. In the Turkish stratum persons with worse health status filled out questionnaires significantly more often and in the German stratum those who are (very) satisfied with the health care system (see Table 4.1).

Our multivariate models predicting participation show similar associations as our bivariate analyses for socio-demographic variables. As can be seen from Table 4.2, for the German stratum the effects of sex, age and marital status persist and explain a variation of 6% (r^2:0.06). For the whole sample, a strong association between nationality and participation can be seen additionally and an explained variation of 14% is reached (r^2: 0.14). Within the Turkish stratum, on the other hand, only persons being in the age of 46 to 55 years were significantly more likely to participate compared to those aged 20 to 35 years (r^2: 0.01). Comparing all three models, it can be seen that hardly any variation in participatory behaviour for the Turkish stratum is explained by the given variables.

Table 4.3 shows binary logistic regression models predicting participation for those who reacted to the questionnaire at all – either by sending back the filled questionnaire or a filled declaration of non-participation (n=1,296). In this group, nationality is not a significant predictor, but the tendency that Turkish nationals are less likely to take part remains. Contrary to bivariate analyses, women are less likely to fill out a questionnaire than men in the models for the whole sample and for the German stratum when adjusting for health related variables. For all three models the biggest effects occurred when contrasting those with 0 to 6 visits to the doctor in the last 12 months with those having been there 7 to 12 or more than 12 times. In the German stratum persons with (very) good health were more likely to take part in the study. All three models explain about 11% of the variation (r^2 for whole sample: 0.11; r^2 for Turkish stratum: 0.11; r^2 for German stratum: 0.12).

Table 4.2. Binary logistic regression models predicting participation (vs. no participation) in the whole sample and both strata

PREDICTOR		WHOLE SAMPLE n=3942			TURKISH STRATUM n=1940			GERMAN STRATUM n=1984		
			aOR	95%-CI		aOR	95%-CI		aOR	95%-CI
Nationality	German	1984	Reference							
	Turkish	1940	0.3	0.2 – 0.3						
Sex	Male	1968	Reference		1000	Reference		968	Reference	
	Female	1956	1.3	1.1 – 1.5	940	1.2	0.9 – 1.5	1016	1.4	1.2 – 1.7
Age	20-35	1349	Reference		796	Reference		553	Reference	
	36-45	1016	1.3	1.0 – 1.6	594	1.3	0.9 – 1.8	422	1.3	0.9 – 1.7
	46-55	945	1.7	1.3 – 2.1	367	1.6	1.1 – 2.3	578	1.8	1.3 – 2.4
	56-65	614	2.0	1.6 – 2.6	183	1.1	0.7 – 1.9	431	2.5	1.8 – 3.4
Marital status	Married	2606	Reference		1401	Reference		1205	Reference	
	Single	378	0.7	0.6 – 0.9	168	1.0	0.6 – 1.5	210	0.6	0.5 – 0.9
	Divorced/Widowed	940	0.8	0.7 – 1.0	371	0.9	0.6 – 1.4	569	0.8	0.6 – 1.1
Urbanity	Urban	1005	Reference		668	Reference		337	Reference	
	Semi-urban	2020	1.0	0.9 – 1.2	1099	1.0	0.7 – 1.3	921	1.1	0.8 – 1.4
	Rural	899	1.1	0.9 – 1.4	173	1.5	0.9 – 2.2	726	1.1	0.8 – 1.4

Table 4.3. Binary logistic regression models predicting participation (vs. declaration of non-participation) in the whole sample and both strata

PREDICTOR		WHOLE SAMPLE			TURKISH STRATUM			GERMAN STRATUM		
		n = 1296	aOR	95%-CI	n=359	aOR	95%-CI	n=937	aOR	95%-CI
Nationality	German	937	Reference							
	Turkish	359	0.7	0.5 - 1.0						
Sex	Male	561	Reference		170	Reference		391	Reference	
	Female	735	**0.6**	**0.4 - 0.8**	189	0.8	0.5 - 1.4	546	**0.5**	**0.4 - 0.7**
Age	20-35	211	Reference		130	Reference		81	Reference	
	36-45	313	0.9	0.6 - 1.4	117	1.2	0.7 - 2.3	196	0.7	0.4 - 1.3
	46-55	379	1.3	0.8 - 2.0	82	1.8	0.8 - 3.8	297	1	0.5 - 1.8
	56-65	278	1.4	0.8 - 2.5	30	0.5	0.5 - 3.9	248	1.2	0.6 - 2.3
Marital status	Married	908	Reference		273	Reference		635	Reference	
	Single	126	0.8	0.5 - 1.3	33	0.7	0.3 - 1.7	93	0.9	0.5 - 1.6
	Divorced/Widowed	262	1.4	0.9 - 2.2	53	2.1	0.9 - 4.7	209	1.1	0.6 - 1.9
Urbanity	Urban	262	Reference		116	Reference		146	Reference	
	Semi-urban	644	1.1	0.7 - 1.6	199	1.2	0.7 - 2.1	445	1.0	0.6 - 1.7
	Rural	390	1.2	0.8 - 1.9	44	1.3	0.6 - 3.1	346	1.2	0.7 - 2.1
Self-rated health	(Very) Good	856	Reference		204	Reference		652	Reference	
	Moderate/(Very) Bad	440	0.8	0.6 - 1.1	155	1.4	0.8 - 2.5	285	**0.6**	**0.4 - 0.9**
Satisfaction with health care service	(Very) Satisfied	796	Reference		191	Reference		605	Reference	
	Moderate/(Very) Unsatisfied	500	0.9	0.6 - 1.2	168	1.2	0.7 - 2.1	332	0.7	0.5 - 1.1
Number of visits to the doctor	0 to 6	703	Reference		204	Reference		499	Reference	
	7 to 12	347	**2.3**	**1.6 - 3.3**	85	**2.3**	**1.2 - 4.6**	262	**2.3**	**1.5 - 3.6**
	>12	278	**5.8**	**3.3 - 10.1**	70	**3.7**	**1.6 - 8.5**	176	**8.1**	**3.7 - 17.4**

Discussion

With our survey, we intended to gain a representative picture of health care utilisation patterns of both, Turkish and German nationals, aged between 20 and 65 years and living in Rhineland-Palatinate. We reached an overall net response rate of 27.7%. It was 14.9% for the Turkish and 40.5% for the German stratum. Whereas the response rate for the German stratum can be considered as satisfactory, the response rate for Turkish nationals is quite low. Since this could be expected from previous research (Blohm & Diehl, 2001; Schenk & Neuhauser, 2005), they were oversampled anticipant. Nonetheless, there is a high risk for selection bias in that sample.

Results of our bivariate analyses for both strata suggest that more married persons answered the questionnaire than those who are single or divorced/widowed. For the German stratum we also see a slight overrepresentation of women and those aged over 35 years. Differing from other studies (Blohm & Diehl, 2001; Nummela et al., 2011), we could not find an association between urbanity of the place of residence and participation in one of the strata or between sex and participation in the Turkish strata. In multivariate analyses, with the data available we could only explain 1% respectively 6% of the variation in participation for the Turkish and German strata, showing that only very low systematic participation bias can be measured. The models depict that nationality was the major predictor of participation next to older age and – in the German stratum being female and married. Furthermore we found that persons visiting the doctor more often were significantly much more likely to take part in the survey, considering only those persons that reacted to the questionnaire. Since women and older persons visit the doctor more often (Thode, Bergmann, Kamtsiuris & Kurth, 2005), the differences in participation decisions by sex, age and doctors' visits might be explained by concern and interest in the topic.

At the same time, persons with better health participated more often in the German stratum. In bivariate analyses this was also true for the Turkish stratum. Unfortunately, we do not have information on health and health care related data for persons not reacting to the questionnaire. Nonetheless, the results might hint to a slight overrepresentation of persons with better health.

Further biases according to socio-economic status and literacy are probable. Additionally, the study design only allows for participation of persons officially registered. This excludes for example homeless persons and those without residence title, who face major obstacles in access to health care. These limitations have to be taken into account when interpreting further results of the study. However, further research explaining participation behavior of Turkish immigrants in bilingual written surveys is necessary, in order make better assumptions on representativeness of survey results and to show better and feasible ways of reaching this subpopulation.

Although the representativeness of the sample is limited, the survey can help finding out more about socio-cultural patterns of health care utilisation, since it is one of very few studies on the topic that is not restricted to people visiting a special medical facility, but instead is a random population sample on two national groups.

Chapter 5: Turkish-language ability of children of immigrants in Germany[1]

Nicole Biedinger, Birgit Becker and Oliver Klein

In the 1960s, German industry was in need of low-skilled labour and started to recruit 'guest workers' (Crul and Vermeulen 2003: p. 970). Many of these labour migrants came from Turkey. In 2011, about 1.6 million individuals of Turkish origin lived in Germany, constituting that country's largest migrant group (Statistisches Bundesamt, 2011). Several studies report that on average, the socioeconomic status of Turkish immigrants is lower than that of native Germans. Furthermore, they are the least well integrated migration group in Germany (Diehl & Schnell, 2006). Research in Germany mainly focuses on the German language ability, but knowledge of the heritage language can help to maintain the immigrants' ties to their ethnic culture, which in turn can facilitate their psychological adjustment. The stronger roots in the ethnic culture may facilitate their social and cultural adjustment through the ethnic community and may also facilitate their adjustment to the host culture (cf. Park et al., 2012). In the following paper we seek to answer the question of how children of Turkish immigrants in Germany are able to learn their heritage language (language retention/maintenance).

Language development follows the same pattern for bilingual as for monolingual children (Clark 2001). The literature on language acquisition is highly developed despite differences in details and emphases: Depending on their academic origin, these models show

---

[1] This chapter is a shorter and previous version of the article: Biedinger, Nicole, Birgit Becker, and Oliver Klein. (Forthcoming). "Turkish-language ability of children of immigrants in Germany: Which contexts of exposure influence preschool children's acquisition of their heritage language?" Ethnic and Racial Studies. http://dx.doi.org/10.1080/01419870.2015.1005641.

great similarities with respect to their main determinants (Chiswick & Miller, 1995; Klein & Dimroth, 2003). In all of these theories and models exposure to language seems to be most important. Exposure to a language can take place in very different settings or contexts (cf. Hoff, 2006). The most important one, particularly for preschool children, is the family. However, the preschool context itself might also be important for language development. Other potentially influential contexts could be media or friends. Nonetheless, for young children of immigrants the family should provide the most intensive area of input to their heritage language, given the much lower probability of contact to the minority language outside the family.

Literature review on contexts of exposure

Results on children's vocabulary acquisition from various linguistic studies verify that children's vocabulary development strongly depends on *parental language input*. It has been shown that the quantity of parental language input (Huttenlocher et al., 1991), as well as the variety and complexity of the language input have positive effects on children's vocabulary acquisition (Pan et al., 2005). Thus, for children of immigrants who grow up bilingually, it is not only the total quantity of language input that matters, but also the proportion of exposure to each language.

Most children also spend some time outside their homes and engage in activities without their parents. For example, they attend *preschools*, are members of sports or music clubs, or go to playgroups. These contexts outside the family can have an independent effect on children's language abilities. Here, especially early educational institutions can be important. Various studies have shown that preschool attendance positively affects children's language skills (Currie & Thomas, 1995; Sammons et al., 2004). However, all of these studies are concerned with the development of the majority language.

In addition, other contexts are also important for early language acquisition. At the time when children come into contact with *peers,* they also influence each other. This can mainly be shown through

60

studies of classroom climate, where the intellectual conditions of the class are very important for children (Downer & Pianta, 2006). Although the studies focus on diverse competencies, most show that peer achievement has a positive effect and that children benefit from higher-achieving schoolmates (Hanushek et al., 2001).

Further, *media consumption* has an influence on the language development. Mendelsohn et al. (2010) suggest that media-verbal interactions may have a direct positive impact on language development, and that media-verbal interactions during the co-viewing of media with educational content were predictive of 14 month-old children's language skills, independently of the overall level of cognitive stimulation in the home (Mendelsohn et al., 2010, also see Tomopoulos et al., 2010).

Data and measures

The empirical analysis is based on data collected in the project "Preschool Education and Educational Careers among Migrant Children" at the University of Mannheim. This projects aims to follow up parents of preschool children aged 3-4 years to the time when they start primary school. The following analysis is based on data from about 450 Turkish-origin families, after excluding cases with missing values.

The subtest 'expressive vocabulary' from the 'Kaufman Assessment Battery for Children' (K-ABC) is used as a measure of *Turkish-language proficiency* because the same subtest was administered to all Turkish-origin children in both languages (German and Turkish). In this subtest, children were shown pictures of objects and asked to name the objects. The name of the object had to be given in Turkish, although the test instructions could be stated in either German or Turkish. The number of correct answers on that subtest is used as dependent variable. The number of right answers can range between 0 and 24.

Exposure to the Turkish language

1) *Family exposure:* First, we use one variable measuring the Turkish language ability of the parents. This is created by the mean of two questions on the self-reported parental proficiency in Turkish. The variable is coded such that higher values indicate a higher proficiency in the Turkish language; second, the frequency of use of the Turkish language is asked; third, we employ a similar question pertaining to communication when friends or relatives visit the family.

2) *Preschool exposure:* First, a variable of duration of preschool attendance in hours since starting to attend kindergarten is created. Second, we use the proportion of Turkish children within each preschool (range from 0 (no Turkish children) to 10 (nearly all children have a Turkish migration background).

3) *Media exposure:* First, we have information about the language of television that the child mainly consumes; second we asked the number of Turkish books within the family (range 0-1,000).

4) *Social contact exposure:* First, we use the proportion of Turkish friends in the social network of the target child: Think about the friends of [target child's name], with whom he/she plays together. How many of those children are Turkish?; second, we also consider the proportion of *Turkish friends* of the parents which is measured with the same answer categories.

Controls

Child's cognitive skills: As a measure of the child's cognitive skills, different subtests of the K-ABC, measuring different cognitive skills are used (gestalt closure, face recognition, number recall). The test instructions as well as the child's answers could be given in either German or Turkish, so there is no Turkish language ability necessary to master these exercises. For each subtest the proportion of correct answers is calculated. Since all three subtest scores load only on one factor in a principal component factor analysis (eigenvalue: 1.71 in the first wave, 1.81 in the second wave, 1.77 in the third wave), this factor score is used in each wave.

Families' socio-economic situation: We use the respondents' educational level as an indicator for the families' socio-economic status. The variable measures the years of education ranging from 1-13years.

Children: Number of children in the family.

Age: Age of the child in months.

Girl: Sex of the child (1: girl; 0: boy)

Because the dependent variable is a metric variable, all cross-sectional models will be done by OLS regression. The last set of results attempts to answer how different levels of exposure affect the development of Turkish language ability over time. To answer this we will calculate fixed-effects models to see if the influence of exposure on the Turkish language ability exists through preschool ages (Allison, 1994).

Results

Table 5.1 show the results of OLS-regressions to explain the influence of different contexts of exposure for the children being 3-4 years old. The results are rather similar for the waves of the older children. The first models show that the child's cognitive skills are most important to explain the Turkish-language ability of the children. Moreover, the parents' education has a negative influence. This might be the case because higher educated parents with a Turkish migration background might assume that learning Turkish is not as important compared to learning German.

In the second model, the language exposure within the family is controlled. The Turkish language ability of the parents has a significant positive influence. The Turkish conversation frequency has a significant influence on the child's ability to speak Turkish. So the influence of family exposure on the Turkish language ability of the child is strong.

Table 5.1. Explaining Turkish-language ability (first wave, children aged 3-4, OLS-Regression).

	1	2	3	4	5	6
Child's cognitive skills	0.13*	0.19***	0.13*	0.13*	0.16**	0.18***
	(0.32)	(0.28)	(0.32)	(0.30)	(0.30)	(0.27)
Parents' years of education	-0.12*	-0.04	-0.08	-0.09+	-0.02	-0.01
	(0.08)	(0.07)	(0.08)	(0.08)	(0.08)	(0.07)
Number of children	0.02	0.00	0.02	0.01	0.01	0.01
	(0.19)	(0.16)	(0.19)	(0.19)	(0.19)	(0.16)
Age in months	0.02	-0.02	0.09	0.03	0.02	0.05
	(0.05)	(0.05)	(0.06)	(0.05)	(0.05)	(0.05)
Girl	0.00	-0.03	-0.01	-0.01	-0.01	-0.04
	(0.36)	(0.32)	(0.36)	(0.36)	(0.34)	(0.32)
Parent's Turkish-language ability		0.24***				0.23***
		(0.27)				(0.27)
Frequency of Turkish in family		0.23***				0.16**
		(0.24)				(0.24)
Frequency of Turkish with relatives		0.12+				0.06
		(0.25)				(0.26)
Duration of preschool			-0.14*			-0.10+
			(0.27)			(0.24)
Proportion Turkish children in preschool			0.14**			0.08+
			(0.08)			(0.08)
Turkish television				0.23***		0.14**
				(0.16)		(0.15)
Turkish books				0.13**		0.08*
				(0.01)		(0.01)
Turkish friends of the child					0.22***	0.08
					(0.19)	(0.15)
Turkish friends of the parents					0.20***	0.04
					(0.15)	(0.22)
Number of cases (N)	405					
R^2	0.03	0.24	0.06	0.10	0.15	0.29

Source: "Preschool Education and Educational Careers among Migrant Children"

Note: Standardized *coefficients with standard errors in parentheses,* + p<0.10; * p<0.05; ** p<0.01; *** p<0.001.

In the third model the impact of preschool is analysed. The duration of preschool attendance has a negative influence on the

Turkish-language ability, but the proportion of other Turkish children within the preschool has a positive influence throughout the whole period. The power of explanation of model three is much lower than in the second model including parental exposure and the additional explanatory power in comparison with the first model that is also very low. The fourth model controls for media exposure. In essence, Turkish television consumption and the availability of Turkish books in the family are positively associated with the Turkish-language ability of children. The fifth model controls for the influence of exposure via friends and social contacts. The results are rather similar: Turkish friends of the child and partly also Turkish friends of the parents have a significant influence on the Turkish-language abilities of the child. Model 6 now controls for all areas of exposure simultaneously.[2] This model confirms the importance of the family context.

Furthermore it is also important to investigate how the changes in contexts of exposure influence the development of the Turkish-language ability over the years. Therefore fixed-effects models were estimated (Table 5.2). The models are organized as before. Model 1 already shows that 21% of the variance in the change in children's Turkish language ability can be explained by the control variables (time-varying) and via the assumption of FE-models also for all time-invariant control variables. Models 2 to 5 do not add much explanatory power.[3] However, the influence of Turkish frequency is almost significant ($t=1.54$; $P>|t|=0.12$) at model 2. Model 3 is also slightly different from the OLS regressions, because the proportion of Turkish children could not be added, therefore an interaction of this variable with the duration was added to control for the ethnic composition. In the last model only the change in family exposure significantly influences the Turkish language ability of the child. Obviously there exist some time-constant variables which explain the Turkish-language

---

[2] In all models we checked for multicollinarity, but the variance inflation factor (vif) was always below 2, so we have no problem of multicollinarity in any reported model.

[3] This may be caused by the fact that fixed effect models bases only on the within variance and this often leads to lower explanatory power and less significant results.

ability. Nevertheless the influence of family is still there, which shows that this area of exposure is very important.

Table 5.2. Explaining the development Turkish-language ability fixed effects.

	1	2	3	4	5	6
Child's cognitive skills	0.42*** (0.05)	0.42*** (0.35)	0.46*** (0.05)	0.42*** (0.05)	0.42*** (0.05)	0.45*** (0.05)
Age in months	-0.07+ (0.04)	-0.06 (0.04)	-0.06 (0.04)	-0.07+ (0.04)	-0.08+ (0.04)	-0.05 (0.04)
Parent's Turkish-language ability		0.07 (0.04)				0.07+ (0.04)
Frequency of Turkish in family		0.04 (0.04)				0.05 (0.04)
Frequency of Turkish with relatives		-0.02 (0.04)				-0.02 (0.04)
Duration of preschool			-0.07 (0.05)			-0.07 (0.04)
Proportion Turkish children in preschool			-0.03 (0.05)			-0.03 (0.05)
Turkish television				-0.01 (0.03)		-0.00 (0.03)
Turkish books				0.01 (0.03)		0.00 (0.03)
Turkish friends of the child					-0.05 (0.04)	-0.05 (0.04)
Turkish friends of the parents					-0.01 (0.04)	-0.02 (0.04)
Number of cases N	1233					
R^2 (within)	0.21	0.21	0.22	0.21	0.21	0.22

Source: "Preschool Education and Educational Careers among Migrant Children"

Note: Standardized *coefficients with standard errors in parentheses*, + $p<0.10$; * $p<0.05$; ** $p<0.01$; *** $p<0.001$.

Conclusion and discussion

Most of the previous research focused on the German-language ability of those immigrants; however, it is also interesting and important to know how their children, who are being raised in Germany and are attending German (pre)schools, are able to learn their heritage language. Therefore the paper has tried to answer the question as to which determinants are most important in order for such preschool children in Germany to learn Turkish. Based on different theoretical models, exposure seems to be most important. Exposure can occur in very different settings, such as within the family, during preschool, via media or through peers. Exposure in general has a very important influence on the language ability of young immigrant children. The main influence is of course through the parents and their own Turkish-language ability. This leads to the implication that promotional efforts should not be limited to just one area. For example, programmes to help young children improve their language ability should start not only at preschool, but also within the family. In contrast the influence of media might be low at this early age, but its influence might increase when the children are old enough to read by themselves and watch more television.

Unfortunately there are some difficulties we have to consider when interpreting our results. First, the group of Turkish immigrants is rather special because they are the biggest group in Germany and have the biggest disadvantages. Unfortunately the data include no information about other ethnic groups. Our results therefore should be replicated with other, and also with smaller immigrant groups. Second, all variables of exposure are measured in a quantitative way, so that we have no information about the quality of the exposure (e.g. we do not know what kinds of TV programmes those children watch; we just know how often they do so). Last, although our data are unique in that they measure the heritage-language ability of immigrant preschool children in Germany, a multidimensional language assessment (e.g. including grammar and other language dimensions) would be very useful. Nevertheless, our results confirm the importance of exposure and different contexts of exposure on language abilities.

Chapter 6: *'Making the balance: to stay or not to stay?'* Highly educated Turkish migrants, trends of migration and migration intentions.

Işık Kulu-Glasgow

For more than a decade the countries of the European Union (EU) have been chasing their ambition to make Europe a 'centre of excellence'. In 2000 they formulated their common goal of making the EU the most competitive and dynamic knowledge economy of the world in the Strategy of Lisbon. The European Recovery Plan of the European Commission, which aimed to combat the most recent economic crisis, emphasized the importance of the innovative knowledge economy and scientific research (European Parliament, 2010). To fulfil the targets of the Europe 2020 Strategy (e.g. increasing productivity, competitiveness, economic growth, solving the problem of labour shortage in sectors of innovation), stimulating intra EU-labour mobility or needs-based migratory flows were named as relevant policy tools.[1] Similarly, encouraging highly skilled[2] immigration from non-EU countries was considered to be essential. In the EU, the share of the highly educated among migrants born outside the EU was almost negligible - only 2% - compared with 4.5% in the USA, 8% in Australia and almost 10% in Canada.[3] As a consequence, the EU-countries got engaged in a global 'battle for brains', not only as a union, but at the same time among themselves in order to attract the 'best and the brightest' and to reach sustainable economic growth.

---

[1] www.ec.europa.eu/commission_2010-2014/andor/headlines/news/2011/07/20110713 _en.htm.

[2] In this paper, the terms 'highly skilled migration' and 'knowledge migration' are used interchangeably.

[3] www.ec.europa.eu/commission_2010-2014/andor/headlines/news/2011/07/20110713 _en.htm.

Within this context, the Dutch government also defined the goal to be a dynamic knowledge economy and to have a strong position in the international 'battle for brains' (Letter of the State Secretary for Justice to the Dutch Parliament, 2007-2008).[4] The ambition was to be one of the leading knowledge economies in the world by capturing a top position in the Global Competitiveness Index[5] (Letter of the Minister of Education, Culture and Science to the Dutch House of Representatives, 2009).[6] The new Dutch immigration policy, the so-called Modern Migration Policy, was seen as a 'business-card' for highly skilled immigrants and international students (idem).[7]

This paper focuses on the case of highly skilled Turkish[8] migration in the Netherlands: 1) Turkish knowledge workers belong to the top-ten nationalities in this type of immigration to the country. 2) At the same time recent research shows that two-thirds of the emigrants who are leaving or (potential immigrants who have the intention to leave) the Netherlands, are of migrant origin, among them highly educated young Turkish men and women (Klaver et al., 2010). A combination of push and pull factors, but mainly better employment opportunities in Turkey, and an increasingly hardening Dutch political climate and growing intolerance for non-western migrants were given as the cause by this group. Some Dutch political parties considered this development as an important loss of human capital in times of a pressing need for knowledge workers in the country and invited the

---

[4] TK 2007-2008, 30573, nr. 10

[5] The Global Competitiveness Index is calculated annually by the World Economic Forum. The Index reflects the concurrence power of the countries in 12 different areas (pillars) such as infrastructure, macro-economic environment, labor-market efficiency, higher education and training, and innovation (http://reports.weforum.org/global-competitiveness-report-2014-2015/).

[6] TK brief ministerie van Onderwijs, Cultuur en Wetenschap, kenmerk: kennis/2009/152087).

[7] The Modern Migration Policy was accepted by the Dutch Parliament in 2010, but was enacted per June 1, 2013.

[8] In this paper, the term 'Turkish' migrants are used for narrative purposes and refers to all migrants from Turkey with different ethnic backgrounds.

government to take the necessary precautions.[9] Similar trends for the emigration of highly educated Turkish populations were also reported in other EU-countries such as Germany, France, Belgium, and Austria.[10] These facts led to some controversy in the mass media that there could be a massive emigration of highly skilled Turkish labour, including the second generation from the Netherlands.

This paper discusses Turkish highly skilled migration by using a triangulation of methods and data sources. Firstly, a brief description of a few Dutch policy instruments to attract highly skilled migrants from non-EU countries is given. Where data are available background characteristics of the highly educated migrants, including Turkish, making use of these different policy measures are presented. Secondly, trends in the immigration and emigration of the highly educated Turkish population to and from the Netherlands are presented. Trend data are based on the registers of the Statistics Netherlands (CBS). Thirdly, intentions of the Turkish highly skilled immigrants regarding their future stay in the Netherlands and factors underlying these intentions are discussed within the context of the value-expectancy model of De Jong & Fawcett (1981). Results in that section are based on qualitative data, which originate from a web survey that has been conducted in May and June 2013 by the Dutch Research and Documentation Centre (WODC). The web survey was held for the evaluation of a recent Dutch policy measure to attract top-talents from non-EU countries, the so-called 'Orientation Year for Highly Educated Persons (Kulu-Glasgow et al. 2014) (see further for the description of the scheme). The survey aimed at those migrants who made use of this scheme between January 1, 2009 and mid-April 2013, and who were still living in the Netherlands. The response rate was 37%, resulting in 100 respondents.[11] The resulting response group was representative for

---

[9] Volkskrant, 28 January, 2011.
[10] NRC, 18 November, 2010.
[11] Between January 1, 2009 and mid-April 2013, 465 people participated in the Orientation Year for Highly Educated Persons Scheme. However, it was not possible to reach all of these participants, as some of them had already left the Netherlands or were not living any more at their last known address. This resulted in a sample of 270 participants (Kulu-

top-ten nationalities, sex and age of all participants who made use of this scheme between January 1, 2009 and December 31, 2012. Turkish migrants are among the top-ten nationalities that made use of this scheme in the Netherlands, as well as in the web survey (5% of the total participants of the Scheme and 8% of the respondents of the web survey).

The analyses suggest that the intention to stay in the Netherlands (or move back to Turkey) is especially driven by other factors than 'classical' economic pull factors. Conclusions are drawn from the results presented in the final section.

Examples of the Dutch policy instruments to attract highly educated migrants

In order to obtain a top position in the 'battle for brains', the Netherlands has been implementing various policy instruments to attract the 'best and the brightest' migrants from non-EU countries. The most important (c.q. widely used) instrument is the Highly Skilled Migrants Scheme.[12] This measure finds its roots at the time soon after the Lisbon Strategy was formulated. Since 2004 migrants from non-EU countries who have a labour contract with an employer situated in the Netherlands can receive a residence permit in the country. The residence permit is given for a year, which can be extended for five consecutive years. After that period, one can apply for permanent residence or naturalization. In order to be considered a highly skilled migrant, one must earn a certain amount of gross monthly salary that is age-dependent. Participants who are younger than 30 years are recognized as a highly-skilled worker with a lower salary than their

---

Glasgow-2014). A recent web survey conducted among highly skilled migrants in the Netherlands had a response rate of 31% (Berkhout et al, 2010).

[12] It is not the aim of this paper to present a description of all the policy measures to attract highly skilled migrants. The section presents three schemes that are either widely used or recent. For a full description of all the measures, see e.g. Obradović, 2013.

older counterparts.[13] The Netherlands is the only EU-country that implements an age-dependent salary criterion for the highly skilled migrants scheme, which is meant to attract young knowledge workers too (Letter of the State Secretary of the Dutch Ministry of Security and Justice and the State Secretary of the Ministry of Social Affairs and Employment, July 1, 2014). According to the national monitors of knowledge workers of the Dutch Immigration and Naturalization Service, between 2008 and 2011 an average of 6,000 non-EU knowledge workers immigrated to the Netherlands under this scheme – more than 23,000 in the whole period - (Obradović, 2013). Turkish migrants are among the top-five nationalities (see Figure 6.1).[14] In general, it is mostly men who make use of this scheme; this is also the case for Turkish migrants (about 80% of the Turkish participants are men) (idem). In spite of the certain amount of salary one has to earn, the highly skilled migrants scheme is considered to be a low-threshold measure.

The most recent Dutch policy measure, enacted on January 1, 2009, is the Orientation Year for Highly Educated Persons. The scheme is designed specifically to attract young 'top-talents' from non-EU countries to the Netherlands *and* to keep them in the Netherlands, for the benefit of the Dutch knowledge economy. Non-EU citizens who obtained a Master's or PhD degree in the Netherlands or from one of the top 200 universities in the world[15], within three years after their graduation can apply for a residence permit to look for a job in the Netherlands as a highly skilled worker, or to set up an innovative business.

---

[13] The level of minimum required income is defined annually. In 2014, younger migrants had to earn a monthly gross salary of €3,205.44 to be recognized as a highly skilled worker, while the limit for older migrants was set at € 4,371.84 (www.ind.nl).

[14] According to the most recent figures between 2008 and 2013 there were 36,190 highly skilled migrants in the Netherlands (distribution per nationality not available at the time of finalizing this paper) (Obradović, 2014).

[15] The ranking of the universities are determined annually according to the following indexes: the Times Higher Education World Rankings, the QS World University Ranking, and the Academic Ranking of World Universities of the Shanghai University.

Figure 6.1. Top-ten nationalities, Highly Skilled Migrants Scheme (2008-2011) (numbers)

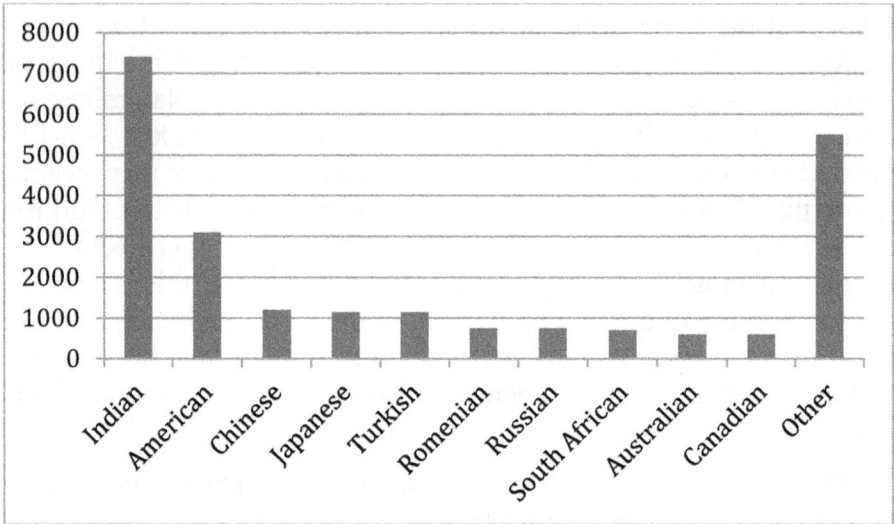

Source: Obradović (2013).

During the search year, participants must finance their own costs of living in the Netherlands. The scheme is based on a points-system.[16] The residence permit for the search year under this scheme is issued for one year only and is not extendable. One must either apply for a change in the purpose of stay (e.g. to work as a knowledge worker, to reside with a partner) or leave the country. To be recognized as a knowledge worker and change the purpose of their stay in this way, participants of

---

[16] To be able make use of the search year under the Orientation Year for Highly Educated Persons scheme one must obtain at least 35 points. Points are awarded as follows: PhD degree, 30 points; Master's degree, 25 points; in following cases the candidates can acquire 5 points: age between 21 and 40 years; previous stay in the Netherlands for work or study purposes; speaking Dutch or English; having obtained the diploma in a country that has signed the Bologna Declaration (Voorschrift Vreemdelingen 2000, bijlage 10, behorend bij artikel 3.23, tweede lid).

the Orientation Year for Highly Educated Persons need to earn a certain amount of income. This required income-level is *lower* than the one for the Highly Skilled Migrants Scheme, is *not* a precondition to be admitted to the country and is *not* age-dependent.[17] Participants who find a job that offers them a lower salary than the required minimum level to be recognized as a highly skilled migrant must obtain a work-permit, which must be arranged by the employer. The research conducted to evaluate the scheme showed that in 2011 only 57% of the participants asked for a change of purpose of stay during or at the end of the search year (Kulu-Glasgow at al., 2014)[18]. The most common reasons were, succeeding to find a job as a highly skilled migrant during the search year (37% of all the participants) or getting a residence permit to reside with a partner who has been already living in the Netherlands (8% of all participants). In the same year 43% of all non-EU migrants who made use of this scheme did not apply to change their purpose of stay. It can be assumed that they left the Netherlands because they could not find a job during the search year. The research findings showed that the requirement to have a work permit under a certain salary level was experienced as an important obstacle in the access to the Dutch labour market by the participants of this scheme.

Between 2009 and 2012 a total of 462 highly educated migrants from non-EU countries made use of the Orientation Year for Highly Educated Persons. Contrary to the Highly Skilled Migrants Scheme, almost as many women as men participate in the scheme (respectively, 47% and 53%). Turkish top-talents rank as the fourth largest group among the participants (a total of 29 Turkish highly educated migrants made use of this scheme during this period) (see Figure 6.2) (idem).

---

[17] On January 1, 2014, the income level was determined at a minimum of €2,297.16 gross per month (www.ind.nl).

[18] These figures are based on a file-research covering the cases of all migrants who made use of the Orientation Year for Highly Educated Persons Scheme in 2011. The file research was carried out by the Analysis and Information Centre of the Immigration and Naturalization Service (INDIAC).

Figure 6.2. Top ten nationalities, Orientation Year for Highly Educated Persons, (2009-2012) (numbers)

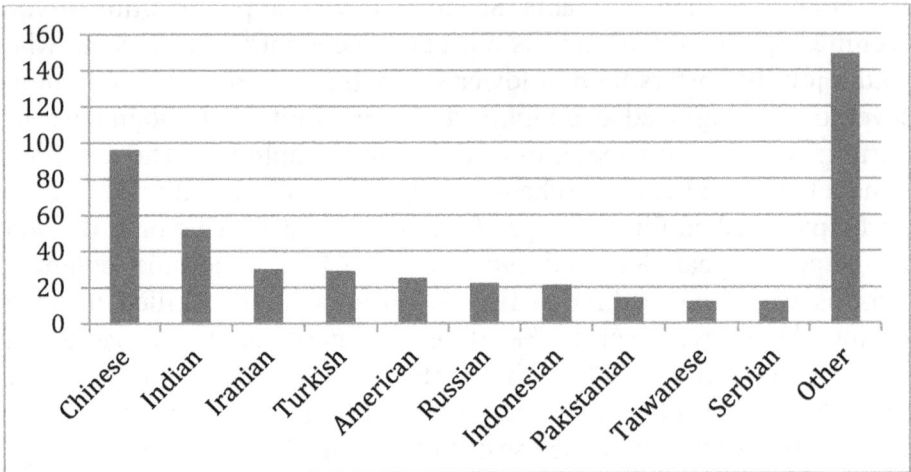

Source: INDIAC

A similar scheme is the Orientation Year for Graduates in the Netherlands. This scheme is meant as a search year for non-EU citizens who have a Bachelor or Master's degree from a Dutch university. The scheme has been implemented since 2004 and aims at keeping international students for the Dutch labour market. Similar to the Orientation Year for Highly Educated Persons scheme, non-EU students can apply for a residence permit that is issued for a maximum of one year to look for a job as a highly skilled migrant in the Netherlands. The application must be done within the first year after graduation or completion of the degree. The required gross monthly salary to be recognized as a highly skilled migrant is equal to the one for Orientation Year for Highly Educated Persons scheme. However, participants of the Orientation Year for Graduates in the Netherlands do not need to acquire a work permit in case they find a job with a lower salary than the required minimum for highly skilled migrants. Highly educated non-EU students can not make use of the Orientation Year for

76

Highly Educated Persons scheme if they had already participated in the Orientation Year for Graduates in the Netherlands.

Trends of immigration and emigration

Migrants of Turkish origin are one of the largest ethnic communities in the Netherlands. Since the oil crisis in the 1970s marriage migration became the most common form of immigration from Turkey to the Netherlands as options for other forms of migration were relatively more limited (e.g. Lucassen & Penninx, 1997). In recent years, Turkish marriage migration has been decreasing (e.g. Van Huis, 2007; Nicolaas, et al. 2011). The nature of recent immigration policies of the Dutch government which aimed at decreasing this type of immigration from non-western countries seem to have an influence on migration flows of the young Turkish population (e.g. WODC/INDIAC, 2009; Chotkowski et al., 2014). The role of changing preferences of the Turkish youth in the Netherlands regarding partner choice should also be recognized in determining this trend, however (e.g. Chotkowski et al., 2014). However, marriage migration is still the most important motive for Turkish immigrants. At the same time, policies designed to encourage immigration of highly qualified labour for the benefit of the Dutch knowledge economy seem to have its influences on the type of Turkish immigration to the Netherlands. As presented above, in recent years Turkish migrants belong to one of the top-ten nationalities among highly skilled workers (see Figures 6.1 and 6.2). There are some indications that professional reasons (e.g. possibility of professional development in the Netherlands, international reputation of the Dutch firms and an innovative economy) and socio-economic factors such as wage levels, social security, Dutch culture and living environment in the Netherlands) are the pull-factors for why the Turkish highly educated choose the Netherlands. Push factors such as poor labour market conditions in Turkey or an adverse

77

political situation seem to be less common reasons to immigrate to the Netherlands.[19]

Figure 6.3 presents the trends for immigration and emigration of the young (20-45 years old) Turkish population, and the net migration in the period 1995-2013, based on the register data from the Dutch Statistics Netherlands.[20]

It can be seen that immigration of Turkish young population had an increasing trend (mainly due to marriage migration) between 1995 and 2004. The influence of recent policy measures, especially those concerning marriage migration can be clearly seen in the immigration trends. Between 2003 and 2004, just before the implementation of stricter income and age requirements for marriage-migration (November 2004), immigration of Turkish population between 20-45 years reached its peak (the so-called 'shadow of the future'). While the immigration trough in 2007 can be explained by the introduction of the civic-integration exam in the country of origin[21], the second peak in 2010 can be associated with the abolishment of the stricter income requirement introduced in 2004. The decline in the Turkish immigration between 2010 and 2013 is probably a result of an increase

---

[19] Responses of the participants of Turkish respondents of the web survey held for the evaluation of the Orientation Year for Highly Educated Persons. Pull factors that are named by the Turkish respondents are also the most common reasons for the whole sample.

[20] This age group is used as a proxy for high education, as the Dutch register data is incomplete for education. It is known that about half the emigration from the Netherlands consists of population in these age groups in almost every population group (55% for the Turkish population) (Klaver et al., 2010). Although it is unknown what the percentage of highly educated Turkish migrants in this age group is, there are indications from previous research that this share is probably not negligible. In a study over the emigration motives of highly educated people from the Netherlands, of the 16 Turkish respondents with a secondary education level of higher, 12 had either completed or were busy with a high school/university education (idem).

[21] The civic-integration exam in the country of origin was introduced in the beginning of 2006 and is meant for migrants between 16 and 65 years from non-western countries who have plans to reside in the Netherlands due to family reunion (including marriage migration/family formation) or as spiritual leaders (Wilkinson, Goedvolk, & Van Dieten, 2008).

in the unemployment levels in the Netherlands and the economic crisis of the time (cf. Jennissen, et al., 2014).

Figure 6.3. Trends in immigration and emigration of young (20-45 years old) Turkish migrants (numbers) (1995-2013)

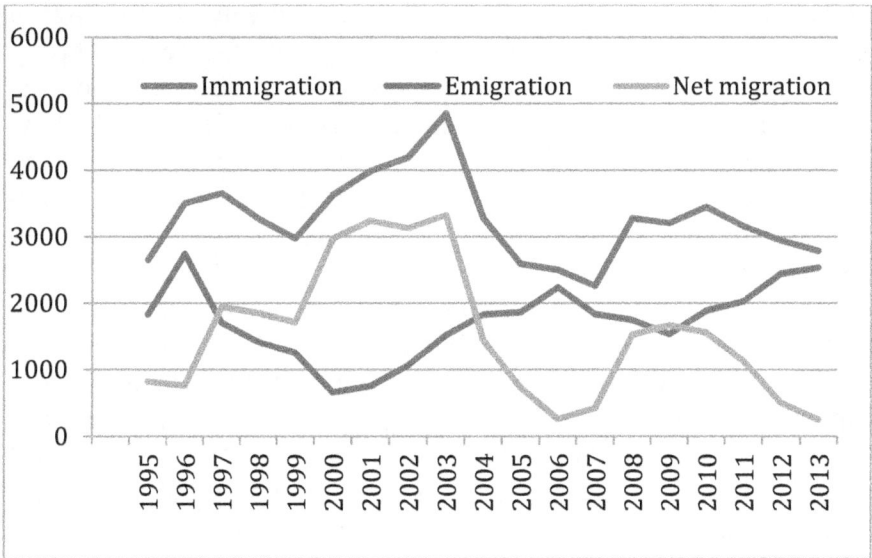

Data: Statistics Netherlands (www.statline.cbs.nl)

With regard to emigration of the young Turkish population, an increase since 2009 can be observed (from about 1500 emigrants in 2009 to 2500 in 2013). Considering these limited numbers it can be argued that there is no massive emigration of young Turkish population from the Netherlands (cf. Klaver et al., 2010). This is also supported by the fact that the percentage of Turkish youth among emigrants between the age group 20-45 is only about 1 to 2% in various years (idem).

The trends in the immi- and emigration of the young Turkish population can be summarized in the trends of net migration. The sharp decrease in immigration and the relative increase in emigration between 2004 and 2007 and after 2010 translate themselves into a steep decline in net migration during these periods. In spite of this sharp decline, the net migration is yet not negative for the Turkish youth in general. Nonetheless, a further break down of the register data shows the following: since 1995 net migration is always positive for the relatively younger Turkish population (age group 20 to 30 years) and in the last decade more often negative for the relatively older (between 30-45 years), illustrating higher levels of emigration for the latter group (data not shown).[22] The results of the above-mentioned study on the emigration motives of highly educated persons in the Netherlands show that a combination of push & pull factors, mainly at macro level, play a role in the emigration of the higher educated Turkish population (20-45 years old). Pull factors seem to be especially essential: Turkish respondents in the study report that they see better chances in Turkey to improve their social and economic position in comparison to the Netherlands. The possibility of having a better job and higher standards of living in Turkey as a result of a growing Turkish economy and possibilities in the Turkish labour-market are given as the concrete reasons to leave the Netherlands (Klaver et al., 2010).[23] The political and social climate in the Netherlands was named as the main push factor: The hardened tone of the public debate on integration of non-western migrants; feelings of segregation of the society into 'us vs. them'; feelings of being not welcome and being set aside as a whole ethnic group; a too individualistic and stressful way of life in the Netherlands were named by the residents of Turkish origin who were considering whether of Turkish origin who were about to, or were considering whether, to emigrate. In addition, micro level factors played a role, such as feeling not completely at home in the Netherlands, presence of family members or a partner in Turkey, and emotional ties with that country (idem).

---

[22] www.statline.cbs.nl

[23] About 40% of the young emigrants migrate to Turkey. Belgium, United Kingdom and Germany are among other countries of immigration (Klaver et al., 2010).

Role of values and expectancies in migration intentions

Classical push-pull theories aim at explaining motives for migration - mostly macro-level defined socio-economic factors. However, such theories are considered to be insufficient in explaining 1) individual decision-making processes, and 2) why while some people migrate, others do *not* (e.g. De Jong & Fawcett, 1981; Freeman, 2012). According to De Jong & Fawcett (1981) improving the quality of life or keeping the status quo is the main reason in the decision to migrate or to stay. The authors assume that the behavior of the individual is determined by his/her beliefs and image-forming, thus it is cognitive. Their value-expectancy model of migration assumes the following: individual motivation cq. intention to migrate is determined by personal goals that people have in life, the values that they attach to each of these goals, and the expectation regarding in which place they can best achieve their most valued goals. The final motivation to migrate or to stay is a subjective, anticipatory weighing of benefits and costs (idem).

De Jong and Fawcett (1981) define seven types of goals that can be of influence on the motivation to migrate or stay:

Comfort: factors related to psychical and psychological comfort (e.g. living in a pleasant/safe environment – respectively for self or for children-; living in a safe society, having a pleasant work environment);

Wealth: factors that have to do with personal economic rewards (e.g. having a good salary, having good welfare benefits);

Status: factors of status and prestige, of which education and occupation are important aspects (e.g. working at a place with an international reputation or working with experts);

Affiliation: factors related to the value of being with others, in relation to, or as a consequence of ,migration (e.g. feeling yourself at home; living close to family & friends);

Autonomy: factors especially related to personal freedom and possibility to live own life, (e.g. living in a tolerant society; having political freedom)

Stimulation: exposure to pleasurable activities (e.g. meeting variety of/new people; having new experiences);

Morality: factors that are related to systems of norms or values, which define what is wrong or what is right, such as systems of religion (e.g. living according to rules of religion).

The model assumes that the strength of the migration intention is the sum of the value-expectancy products related to these respective, individual goals:

$$SI = \sum_{i=1}^{n} (V_i * E_i)$$

The multiplicative assumption exists due to the following reason: if a specific goal has a limited or no value for the individual, or there is little or no expectation that a valued goal can be realized in a particular place, that goal will contribute little or not at all to the total migration intention regarding staying at or leaving that particular place (idem). Previous research shows that migration intentions are good predictors of actual migration behaviour (e.g. De Jong et al., 1983; De Jong, 2000).[24]

Migration intentions and values and expectancies of Turkish top-talents

During the web survey conducted to evaluate the Orientation Year for Highly Educated Persons Scheme, the respondents (n=100) were provided with 19 personal goals following the seven categories of goals

---

[24] The value-expectancy model is applied broadly in social-sciences to explain behaviour. For its applications to explain migration behaviour, see for example, Arnold (1987), De Jong et al. (1983), De Jong et al. (1996), Freeman (2012) en Wentzel et al. (2006).

defined by De Jong & Fawcett (1981). They were requested to score each of these goals with respect to 1) the level of importance of that individual goal to them and 2) to state the country where they see their chances better to achieve that particular goal (better in the Netherlands, better in country of birth, the same in the Netherlands as in the country of birth). As the absolute number of the Turkish respondents is limited, a qualitative analysis is conducted to explore 1) the migration intentions of the highly educated Turkish migrants regarding their future stay in the Netherlands and, 2) values and expectancies that lie behind these intentions (n=8).[25] [26]

All of the Turkish respondents who participated in the web survey had their Master's or PhD degree from a Dutch university. They were all born in Turkey, the majority of them (n=6) were living in Turkey before they migrated to the Netherlands (two respondents were living in another EU country) for study or work purposes. Most of the respondents (n=6) were still living in the Netherlands before they had participated in the scheme to look for a job as a highly skilled worker. At the time of the survey, the majority of the respondents (n=6) were working, where almost all (n=5) earned a salary that is equal or higher than the required minimum to be recognized as a highly skilled worker. Two respondents were looking for a job. Their average years of stay in the Netherlands was 5.5 years.

It should be emphasized that qualitative findings presented below should be treated solely as illustrative. The results can serve as a means of input for future research on migration intentions of Turkish migrants

---

[25] In the evaluation research mentioned, the value-expectancy model was tested for the whole sample quantitatively. Firstly, value-expectancy scores for each of the individual goals were calculated. Consequently, respective composite value-expectancy scores for the seven goals defined by Fawcett & Jong were calculated for the Netherlands and for country of birth (Kulu-Glasgow et al., 2014).

[26] The number of Turkish respondents in the sample is low, but the percentage in the sample is the same, even a little higher than the percentage in the total population who made use of this scheme during the research period (8% vs. 6%).

and should be treated as hypotheses to be tested. They do *not* have any ambition of making a generalization.

When asked about their plans regarding their future stay in the Netherlands, half of the Turkish respondents stated that they intend to stay in the Netherlands in the future (potential stayers) (n=4). The other half had either the intention to emigrate (potential emigrants) (n=2) or was undecided (doubters) (n=2).[27]

There are indications that different goals and expectations underlie the different migration intentions of highly educated Turkish migrants.[28]

Potential stayers

Autonomy related goals (particularly having political freedom and living in a tolerant society) contribute the most to the highly educated Turkish migrants' decisions to stay in the Netherlands in the future: all four highly educated Turkish potential stayers state unanimously that these two goals are their most valued personal goals in life. All of these respondents expect that their chances to achieve these two goals are better in the Netherlands than in Turkey.

Professional status (particularly professional growth), a *comfort* related goal, having a pleasant work environment (having nice colleagues, regular working hours, and a less stressful work environment) and the goal of having good welfare provisions & other economic benefits (wealth) are other goals that contribute to the intention of the highly educated Turkish potential stayers. Almost all the respondents (n=3) expect that their chances of achieving these goals are better in the Netherlands (otherwise, chances are considered to be the same in the Netherlands and in Turkey). It is noteworthy that in the

---

[27] The percentage of the Turkish respondents who intend to stay in the Netherlands is similar to the one for all the respondents in the sample: 52% (potential emigrants 14%, doubters 34% (Kulu-Glasgow et al. 2014).

[28] In the qualitative analysis, personal goals that are considered 'very important' and 'important' are taken into account (most valued goals will contribute the most to choose for a specific country if the person expects to achieve these goals in that country).

general sample, the highest value-expectancy score for potential stayers was for comfort related factors (especially living in a pleasant surrounding to bring up children) (Kulu-Glasgow et al., 2014). It is possible that young highly educated Turkish migrants trade this personal goal for political freedom and tolerance in a society, which they unanimously expect to find in the Netherlands compared to Turkey. Goals related to professional status (particularly working in an environment with an international reputation and with experts), and autonomy (especially living in a tolerant society) were also important in the intention of highly educated migrants from non-EU countries to stay in the Netherlands (idem).

It is notable that having a higher salary, which is considered as one of the 'classical' pull factors of migration, is not as prominent as other goals in determining the migration intentions of the highly educated migrants, including the Turkish. There is evidence that in general, economic factors are more important in the initial decision to immigrate to another country rather than the decision regarding return migration (Finch et al., 2009).

Potential emigrants

For the two Turkish potential emigrants, *professional status* (professional growth) and *affiliation* (having family and friends you can rely on, and feeling yourself at home) are the most valued goals in life ('very important'). These respondents expect that their chances to achieve these goals are either the same in Turkey as in the Netherlands (professional growth) or better in Turkey (affiliation). One of the two respondents states that having a stable employment *(wealth)* is 'very important' for him and that his chances to achieve that is better in Turkey than in the Netherlands. These qualitative findings indicate that affiliation related goals probably contribute the most to the intention of Turkish highly educated migrants to return to Turkey. For the potential emigrants in the general sample the value-expectancy score for affiliation related goals for their country of birth was also the highest. There is evidence that in general, affiliation related factors rather than economic factors are more important in the return migration decisions of migrants (Finch et al., 2009).

Doubters

The two Turkish highly educated respondents who are undecided about their future stay in the Netherlands report various personal goals in life that they value the most. Their expectations regarding the country where they can achieve these individual goals vary, however. They consider that their chances of achieving their most valued *comfort* related goals (particularly living in a nice/pleasant surrounding) are the same in the Netherlands and in Turkey; but think that their chances of reaching their most valued goals related to *wealth* (especially having good welfare provisions and having a good salary), *professional status* (particularly working at a place with international reputation and working with experts), and *autonomy* (having privacy and being able to be on your own) are better in the Netherlands. On the other hand, they expect that they can achieve their other most valued goal, *affiliation*, better in Turkey.

Conclusions

Turkish migrants are one of the largest ethnic communities in the Netherlands. Since the 1970s until recently, marriage migration in the Netherlands is the main source of immigration of the Turkish population. Policies to restrict this type of immigration among non-western migrants in general (and among the Turkish and Moroccan population in particular), and changing partner choice preferences of the second generation of Turkish population in the Netherlands seem to have an influence on the inflow of the young Turkish population. The country's new immigration policy (the so-called Modern Migration Policy) is considered to be an 'invitation card' for the highly skilled migrants. In the last decade, the Dutch government has implemented a series of policy measures to attract 'the best and the brightest' from non-EU countries in the global 'battle for brains'. Highly skilled Turkish immigrants are among the top-ten nationalities. At the same time, in the last few years there has been a sharp increase in the emigration of higher educated Turkish youth who are either born or grew up in the Netherlands. Better chances to improve their socio-economic position as a result of the growing Turkish economy, a negative political and social climate against the non-western migrants, a too individualistic way of life and emotional ties with Turkey are among the emigration reasons. The register data show that absolute numbers of these emigrants cannot be considered as massive; still the net migration for young Turkish population is decreasing. The important question is whether these trends will continue in the future, and lead to a negative net migration for the young Turkish population in the Netherlands.[29]

A recent Dutch policy measure (enacted in 2009) within the context of the Dutch Modern Migration Policy is the Orientation Year for Highly Educated Persons. This scheme aims at *attracting* and *keeping* top-talents who have a Master's or PhD degree from a Dutch university from one of the top 200 universities in the world. Those who make use of this scheme get a residence permit for a maximum period of one year to look for a job in the Netherlands as a highly skilled migrant. Turkish top-talents rank the fourth in numbers among the participants. An evaluation of this scheme showed however that this instrument could only reach a limited number of top-talents, among which there were only 29 Turkish migrants. The requirement of a work permit in some cases and the fact that the scheme probably is not well known internationally are among the bottlenecks (Kulu-Glasgow et al., 2014). The Dutch government is looking for new options to keep the Dutch knowledge economy competitive and attractive for the best and the brightest. There are plans to lift the work permit obligation for a certain group of top talents who participate in the above mentioned scheme (Letter of the State Secretary of Ministry of Security and

---

[29] Due to the nature of the register data the exact share of the highly educated Turkish population among the emigrating young population is unknown.

Justice and State Secretary of Social Affairs and Employment to the Dutch House of Representatives, July 1, 2014).

A web survey conducted among the participants of the Orientation Year for Highly Educated Persons scheme who were still in the Netherlands show that only half of the top talents from non-EU countries intend to stay in the Netherlands in the future. This seems also to be the case for Turkish participants of the scheme. The analyses in this paper suggest that highly educated Turkish potential stayers value personal goals such as having political freedom, living in a tolerant society, professional growth, having a pleasant work environment, and having good welfare provisions and other economic benefits, and see their chances of achieving almost all of these goals better in the Netherlands.

For top talents who intent to return to Turkey, this intention seems to be driven by reasons of affiliation with Turkey (having family and friends you can rely on, and feeling yourself at home) and expectations of better opportunities for professional growth in that country. Both the potential stayers and potential emigrants value professional growth, but have different expectations regarding where their chances are better to achieve this goal. Those who do not have a clear intention of whether to stay in the Netherlands or go to Turkey seem to be divided between their values and expectations regarding a greater number of personal goals such as living in a nice/pleasant surrounding, having good welfare provisions and having a good salary, working at a place with international reputation and working with experts, having privacy and being able to be on your own, and feelings of belonging and living close to family and friends.

The findings suggest that social and political conditions, personal goals related to one's professional life, and ties with the country of origin contribute more to highly educated Turkish migrants' intentions to stay or leave the immigration country, than classical economic pull factors. More quantitative and qualitative research on this topic is recommended. A better understanding of highly skilled migrants' decision-making process can assist European governments to create better conditions that persuade the 'best and the brightest' to stay, to the benefit of their knowledge economies.

Chapter 7: Human capital exchange between Germany and Turkey. A focus on Turkish students in Germany

Rebecca Tlatlik and Beatrice Knerr

Germany is facing a shrinking and ageing population due to a sustained decline of the country's birth rate and a longer life expectancy of its population. As a result, the population is expected to decrease to 70 million in 2030 (BMAS, 2011), from 80.62 million in 2013 (Statistisches Bundesamt, 2014), while the labour force is predicted to drop by 4% between 2010 and 2020 (OECD, 2013a). The German Federal Employment Agency (FEA), moreover, expects a skilled labour deficit of around 5.4 million in 2025 (FEA, 2011). This development preoccupies policymakers as well as business representatives, because the availability of highly qualified human capital is seen as a basis for the country's prosperity (Czernomoriez, 2009). Especially the growing shortage of specialists in the MINT subjects, i.e. Mathematics, Informatics, Natural Science and Technique, might have severe consequences for the economy. In order to find a way to cope with this situation, the attraction of highly skilled people from abroad has come into the focus of German politics. Hence, with the New Immigration Act ("Zuwanderungsgesetz") in 2005, Germany officially accepted its status as an immigration country, and accordingly put a regulatory framework in place. Consequently, the new law and its following modifications made Germany one of the countries with the lowest entry restrictions to the domestic labor market towards highly-skilled migrants within the OECD area (OECD, 2013a).

In this situation, attracting and retaining international students[1] came into the foreground, because they are "characterized by youth, host-country language ability, full-credential recognition, significant acculturation and domestically relevant professional training" (Hawthorne, 2010:94) and therefore are considered as the ideal labour migrants. Between 2001 and 2011, the total number of foreign students[2] in Germany increased from 187,027 to 282,201, although the country's share in the international students market dropped by almost three percentage points to 6% of the worldwide foreign student population in 2011 (OECD, 2013b). As Germany's immigration policy has become more skill selective since 2005, easier pathways are provided for international graduates from non-EU/EFTA countries (so-called "third-country nationals") to shift from their student status to labour force. To contribute to filling the specific demand of the labour market, graduates are only allowed to stay on if they find a job which fits their qualifications.

In 2013, 10.9% (in total 30,645) of Germany´s foreign students had Turkish citizenship; 78% of them (i.e. 23,979 persons) were educational locals[3] and 22% (6,666 persons) international students (DAAD and DZHW, 2014). Thus, the share of students with Turkish citizenship accounted for 30.9% within the group of educational locals, but just 3.3% within the group of international students enrolled in German universities, which seems surprising taking into account the strong personal networks which exist between both countries - with Germany being the major host country of Turkish emigrants, and Turks constituting the largest immigrant group in Germany. This essentially raises two questions: Is the full potential of Turkish residents in Germany exhausted in the context of alleviating its shortages of skilled labor force? And why are not more international students from Turkey

---

[1] These are students, who have a foreign citizenship and obtained their secondary education abroad. They came to Germany to for pursuing higher education.

[2] This group is composed of educational locals (i.e. persons with non-German nationality who have finished high-school in Germany) and other foreigners.

[3] These are students with foreign citizenship who obtained their secondary education in Germany or at a German school abroad. They mainly grew up in Germany.

choosing Germany as host country for their higher education? Our paper focuses on the Turkish student population and aims to assess their potential to alleviate Germany´s growing shortage of skilled labor force. This is done by a literature review and an analysis of secondary data. The migration of highly skilled persons from Germany to Turkey will also be addressed, with a focus on student mobility.

High skilled migration to Germany

The importance of human capital for the economic growth of countries is well established in economic growth theories (Storper et al., 2009). One of these theories is the human capital theory, where human capital is defined as skills and knowledge embodied in people (Schultz, 1961), and education and training are assumed to raise a worker's productivity (Xiao, 2001). Hence, an insufficient stock of human capital would threaten the prosperity of a country, and Germany, facing a demographic shift towards an ageing and shrinking population, aims to counterbalance its decreasing native human capital by attracting highly skilled foreigners.

In 2012, 305,595 persons from third countries settled in Germany, the three major reasons given for entering being family reunification (17.1%), employment (12.6%) and studying (12.7%). While the number of those coming for family reasons dropped by more than 50% between 2002 and 2012 (from 85,305 to 40,843) yet, the size of the other two groups increased. Since the "New Immigration Act" was implemented in 2005, the number of admissions of non-EU/EFTA citizens for employment (regulated by §18 AufenthG) more than doubled, from 18,415 in 2005 to 38,745 in 2012. Most of the immigrants in this category came from India (12.5%), Croatia (11.5%) and the United States (10.1%), while the share of those with Turkish origin made up just 4.3% (BAMF, 2013). Around 75% (27,349) of the labour migration to Germany in 2012 was for employment requiring skilled or highly skilled qualifications. Migration from India, Japan, Korea, China and Turkey has been characterized by a disproportionately high share of people entering into this labour market segment.

Between 2000 and 2013, the number of international students from non-EU/EFTA countries in Germany increased, from 112,883 to 204,633. In 2012, 30,806 international students graduated, among them 70.6% from third countries. 42.7% of the international students obtained a degree in mathematics, natural sciences or engineering, i.e. subjects which are particularly important for the German labour market. Germany is especially interested in retaining graduates with these qualifications. In 2012, 4,223 international students received a residence permit[4], allowing them to stay in the country for job search after graduation. Most of these permissions were granted to Chinese, Russians, Indians, Ukrainians and Turks. Between 2006 and 2011, the number of foreign graduates who obtained a residence permit because they found an appropriate job[5] increased from 2,742 to 7,392. From January to July 2012, 4,363 international graduates from third countries received a residence permit because they found a job fitting their qualifications, with the largest share (25%) being Chinese. (BAMF, 2013)

Turkish citizens in Germany

Turkish nationals constitute the largest Diaspora in Germany. In 2013, 1,549,808 persons with Turkish citizenship lived in Germany (FSO, 2014). However, since 2000, this group has been decreasing, a major reason being transitions into German nationality. Furthermore, since 2006 more Turkish nationals left the country than the number of those immigrating to Germany (Zeyneloglu & Sirkeci, 2014). For example in 2012, 26,160 Turks moved to Germany while 27,725 left, whereby no systematic empirical information is available about their destinations (BAMF, 2013). While family reunification still was the major reason given by Turkish nationals for entering Germany, the absolute number of this group has decreased from 22,100 in 2003 (29% of all entries) to 7,332 in 2012 (37.5%) (BAMF, 2013 and 2004). The second most important entry reason in 2012 was employment (8%).

---

[4] According to §16 Abs.4 AufenthG
[5] According to §27 Abs.1 Nr.3 BeschV

This category is characterized by a high share of skilled migration (BAMF, 2013). In 2012, 1,473 (4.3%) of the immigrants who obtained an employment permit were Turkish nationals, only a marginal share (2.5%) of them received it for an unskilled job. 7.3% of the Turkish nationals who moved to Germany in 2012 came for studying (BAMF, 2013).

Turkish students in Germany

The number of Turkish students in Germany reached 28,501 in 2012, an increase of 16% compared to 2004. They constituted 10.7% of the total foreign student population and hence were the largest foreign nationality group (DAAD and DZHW, 2013). The vast majority of them were educational locals: in 2012, with a total number of 21,917, they made up 77% of all students with Turkish nationality enrolled in Germany´s higher education system. Between 2008 and 2012 their number increased by 51% and their share among all educational locals increased from 26% to 30.3% (DAAD and DZHW, 2013). The number of graduates among them grew by 42% between 2004 and 2011 to 1,834 (DAAD and DZHW, 2013).

The 10 most chosen subjects of Turkish educational locals in 2010 were economics (19.2%), followed by informatics (10.5%) and mechanical engineering (9.8%). Hence, within these areas, 40.2% studied a subject which is in high demand on the German labor market (DAAD and DZHW, 2012). These figures suggest that Turkish educational locals may play an increasingly important role in Germany´s labour market segment for highly qualified labour force. A major prerequisite to succeed in higher education is the pre-university education of the Turkish youth. Here, the figures about Turkish pupils in the German educational system suggest an unexploited potential: in 2010, just 11% of them went to upper secondary school (Gymnasium), which is a significantly lower share than among other foreign children in the country (14%) and a much lower share than among German pupils (29%) (DAAD, 2012).

In 2012, 3.4% of the international students enrolled in German universities came from Turkey, with their total number remaining almost constant between 2004 (6,474) and 2012 (6,584). In 2012, more Turkish international students (1,491) were enrolled at undergraduate level than at post graduate level (1,105), while their proportion within the student community increased with the degree level: undergraduates constituted 4.2% and postgraduates 5.1% of all students within the ten most chosen subjects. At both levels, Turks were mainly enrolled in subjects, which are in high demand on the German labor market: 80.4% at undergraduate level and 65.7% at postgraduate level (see Table 7.1). At the undergraduate level informatics was the most popular (32.3%), followed by mechanical engineering (29.2%) and electrical engineering (29.2%). At postgraduate level, mechanical engineering (23.3%) was the subject, with the highest proportion of Turkish international students. A similarly high share was enrolled in economics (22.9%), while informatics was the third most chosen subject. Thus, although the average share of students enrolled in these subjects was lower at undergraduate level (42.4%) than at postgraduate level (51.6%), at undergraduate level Turkish international students were more concentrated in subjects, which are in high demand by German companies.

At PhD level, Turkish international students constituted 4.6% of those enrolled in the five most chosen subjects[6] in 2012. Most of them (33.2%) were registered in mechanical engineering (DAAD and DZHW, 2013).

The proportion of Turkish graduates among the international students enrolled in the ten subjects with the most international graduates in 2011, increased with degree level, although at the same time their absolute number dropped due to the fact that less Turkish international students were enrolled at postgraduate and PhD level.

---

[6] Biology, Chemistry, Physics/Astronomy, Mechanical Engineering and Medicine

Table 7.1. Turkish international students within the ten most chosen subjects by international students at undergraduate and postgraduate levels in 2012 (%)

Subject	Undergraduate	Postgraduate	
Economics	n.a.	Economics	22.9
Mechanical Engineering	29.2	Electrical Engineering	15.3
Informatics	32.3	Mechanical Engineering	23.3
Electrical Engineering	18.9	Informatics	15.7
Medicine	n.a.	Music	n.a.
German language	n.a.	German language	3.8
Law	6.9	Law	4.8
Architecture / Interior design	6.8	Construction / Engineering	7.3
Music	n.a.	Engineering	4.1
Education science	5.9	Architecture / Intererior design	2.8

Source: DAAD and DZHW (2013)

Economics was the subject with the most graduated international students at undergraduate level, and also most of the Turkish students (33.1%) obtained a degree in this subject, followed by informatics (23.7%), electrical engineering (15.3%) and mechanical engineering (14.8%). At postgraduate level Turkish students constituted 3.8%. But most of the Turkish students obtained a degree in mechanical engineering (33%), followed by economics (23.3%) and informatics (11.7%). In general, there is a high proportion of Turkish international students who graduate (47.6%) in subjects, which are in high demand. At PhD level in 2011, Turkish students cluster in biology, medicine and mechanical engineering which was the subject in which most Turkish students (24.4%) graduated.

In the winter term of 2012/13 a higher proportion of the total Turkish foreign student population were enrolled in mathematics and natural sciences (20.8%) than Germans (18%). The same applied to engineering, which was chosen by 31.8% of the Turkish students, as compared to just 19.3% of the Germans. Between January and July 2012, the GFEA granted 4,363 permissions for international graduates to take up a job fitting their qualifications. Among them were 4.2% from Turkey (BAMF, 2013).

Turning to the question why not more international students from Turkey can be found at German universities, the answer can be found in the generally low number of Turkish students studying abroad. While in 2012 51,487 mobile Turkish students were abroad, their outbound enrollment ratio was just 0.8% (UNESCO, 2014). At the same time, the networks between Turkey and Germany appear effective in attracting Turkish students to German universities: In 2012, Germany was the major host country of outbound Turkish students with a total number of 12,222, closely followed by the United States with 11,597, then, after a large gap, Bulgaria with 5,015, and the UK with 3,320 (UNESCO, 2014).

Human capital migration from Germany to Turkey

Over the early 21st century, Turkey also has become more attractive for highly skilled migrants from Germany. An indicator for this is the fact that from 1999 to 2004, the number of German students in Turkey more than doubled from 60 to 143 students which was still a comparatively miniscule number. After Turkey joined the ERASMUS program in the academic year 2004/05, the number increased significantly, up to 1,337 German citizens enrolled in Turkey's higher education system (FSO, 2013b), most of them being ERASMUS students (1,231). The number further increased to 1,730 in 2012; 434 started and 134 finished their studies, all with a Bachelor degree. 42.3% were enrolled in law, economics and social sciences, followed by languages, cultural science and sports (31.7%) (FSO, 2013b).

In 2012, Turkey was the fourth most important destination country for migrants from Germany. Around 26,500 German citizens moved to Turkey (BAMF, 2013), but there is only sketchy information available about how far those who migrated to Turkey have Turkish roots. Furthermore, official data does not provide information about the skill level and qualifications of the out-migrants and their possible return.

Conclusion

Due to Germany's emerging labour skill shortage, especially in the MINT subjects, the country welcomes highly skilled labour migrants. In this regard, attracting international students into Germany's higher education system and retaining those with sought- after qualifications after their graduation, is used as a strategy to fill emerging human capital gaps. Turkish nationals constitute the biggest foreign student population in Germany. Educational locals and educational foreigners both displayed a higher inclination than German students to study subjects, which are in high demand by German companies, namely mathematics, informatics, natural sciences, and engineering, and therefore, could enter the skilled labor market and contribute to ease the skill shortages.

Although the number of Turkish foreign students in Germany's higher education system increased, mainly due to more Turkish educational locals, it appears that Germany does not fully exploit the human capital potential of the Turkish community. So far, the proportion of Turkish nationals in Germany, who go to upper secondary school, has been much lower than that of the Germans. In order to increase the number of Turkish educational locals with high school degrees, the share of Turkish pupils first would have to catch up with that of Germans. Therefore, measures should be taken to improve the performance of Turkish nationals in secondary and primary school schools.

Furthermore, the number of international students from Turkey in Germany is stagnating. Although Turkey is only the sixth most important sending country of international students in Germany

(DAAD and DZHW, 2013), Germany is the major host country for Turkish students enrolled abroad, thus demonstrating that the long migration history between both countries is effective in attracting Turkish students to Germany. Turkish students appear to be a valuable resource for Germany's labour market as they are interested in studying MINT subjects and also tend to take up employment in Germany after their graduation. Among the Turkish international student population in Germany are also many ERASMUS students, who usually stay only for a few months and therefore would not directly shift from being an international student to the host country's labour force, but based on their visit may still build up professional ties with Germany later on.

Chapter 8: Identity formation of young second and third generation Turkish-origin migrants in Vienna and their attitude towards integration in Austrian society

Maja Richtermoc

Introduction

This case study chapter explains how self-determination develops in the case of young Austrians with Turkish migration background in Vienna. Through the incorporation of Austrian, as well as the Turkish socio-cultural values and knowledge, members of the investigated population create their own kind of multiple identities that lead to fuller, more successful integration.

There is no common, general definition of identity. The simplest one is that identity is the fact of being who or what a person or thing is. Still, this definition is also not clear due to the "*problems of marginizing and defining of the identity which go back to its multidimensional, dynamic character, that gives the identity its complexity, as well as its flexibility*" (Kalanj, 2008:61). This approach to identity is applicable to the field of cultural studies that sees personal identity as interfering and combining social groups. It forms both plural and contradictory interpretation possibilities that are not taken as critical *per se*, but are understood as normal in the scope of multiple and hybrid identities (Florio-Hansen & Hu, 2007:87). Mesić explains that "*the identiy formation is an active process, based on the bilateral dynamics of inclusion and exclusion. There is no identity without the dialogical relationship with the Other. The concept of "us" exists only in the relation with "others"*" (Mesić, 2006:287).

Just as the sovereignty of the state, people perceive their ethno-cultural background in the same way: it is a form of awareness of oneself that develops only in contact with others. This constantly changing concept creates *"the reflexive project of the self, which consists in sustaining of coherent, yet continuously revised, biographical narratives"* (Giddens, 1991, in: Florio-Hansen, Hu, p.VIII). In the case of second and third generation migrants, this search becomes a form of identity management around the questions of which one, which one of the two, or which third group one should affiliate oneself with (Oswald, 2007:137).

The main problem with integration studies is the lack of consensus concerning what succesful integration means and how it is measured. Austrian integration policy focuses on the stengthening of migrant's chances for education and socio-economic success, as well as the implementation of different initiatives for more inclusion, understanding and xenophobia (Ulram, 2009:7).

In my research, I focused on the subjective factors related to integration awareness that analyse the individual's personal perception of their own integration in the majority of society. It is likely that the sense of belonging increases with the length of stay, so the vast majority of the second and third generation should feel more attached with Austria than with Turkey. Due to the fact that the main difficulties in forming and implementing the most suitable integration policy lie in the philosophy of the nation-state, I, similarily to Maxwell, argue that *"(...) second-generation migrant-origin individuals have grown up in the same environment as migrant-origin individuals and are likely to share the same evaluations of the host society"* (Maxwell 2010:30). It makes migrants members of both societies simultaneously and leads to improved formal integration, followed by the attempt to maintain cultural features of the country of origin. Furthermore, it leads to the developement of the feeling of double belonging, that members of the population see as an enrichment to their personal identity, rather than an obstacle, which at the same time results in easier and more successful integration.

Method

The main goal of the study was understanding the complexity of one social phenomenon, without trying to claim its general validity and statistical relevance.

The research is based on the extensive theoretical analysis of the concepts of identity and integration, the Austrian integration policy and trends during 2011-2013, followed by empirical analysis of nine qualitative interviews with representatives of the investigated population, made by the author, during 2012. They were Austrians with Turkish migration backgrounds from Vienna (second and third generation), predominantly in their early twenties, chosen through the word-of-mouth sampling method. They belong to similar social status and have some sort of higher education degree, since people of that profile are more likely to discuss the topic with stronger sense of self-reflection and awareness of abstract topics such as identity or integration.

The most important questions focused on awareness of their personal identity, their use of languages and perception of their native language, followed by reflection on their place within Austrian society.

Results

Circle of friends as a distinguishing element

Since social background and social contacts have a major influence in the personal developement of an individual, I was wondering if the interviewees would confirm Reckwitz' assertion, that *"(...)in the highly contemporary societies collective identities go above and beyond the functionally differentiating roles of mere social identities and group themselves around collectively shared codes of conduct. Only then, in the context of that conduct, can narrative personal identities be built"* (Reckwitz, 2008:63). The interviews proved this theory to be right and participants' narrow circle of friends appeared to be "multi-culti". Suprisingly, some of them talked about the non-binding nature of their relationships to Turkish migrants: their closest friends were not of

Turkish origin since their attitudes towards politics, religion, way of life and family differed too much from their own. If they did have Turks as friends, those were citizens of the Republic of Turkey who were still living there, cousins and friends, or ones who came to Austria to study. Some of them told me that they *"just don't hit it off with those gürbetçis"* (Richtermoc, 2014:65), even though they themselves belonged to this group.

The interviewees I talked to were fully aware that they do not share the same upbringing as the other children of Turkish immigrants and were grateful to their parents for their efforts, not to put them into the category of Turks in Austria. It is that exact view of the world and political affiliation that one of the participants used to filter out friends among the ones of Turkish origin, while he has no such criteria for the Austrian ones. Another one claims that his good language skills without an accent and his aspirations for higher education were the main reason why he connected more easily and more "naturally" with Austrian pupils. It was by accident that he got to know some Turkish origin friends (in his late teens) which helped him not to lose his knowledge of Turkish.

In addition to parents' role in choosing the (better) school for their children's education, my conversational partners claimed that their upbringing, life values, friends and family, were given to them through the socio-cultural norms and values of their parents' country of origin. Those positive aspects of Turkish mentality shaped them as individuals and their attitude towards what was important in intrapersonal relations with other people.

Education, upbringing and family influence appears to play a key role in creating the course of personal developement of the researched population. Because of the lack of education of first generation migrants, it often happens that the new generations are living in the atmosphere that does not appreciate it as a value and it perpetuates the vicious circle.

The assumption that *"the education-specific hopes that parents have towards their children, are within the Turkish families higher"*

(Bertsch, 2010, p.40) proves to be right. People interviewed stated the necessity for schooling and information exchange, but emphasized the reasons for their success in the ethno-cultural values engrained within the family, especially by enabling them to have a bilingual upbringing. They appreciate their Turkish roots and plan to maintain them further as a part of their personality.

The profile of the Turkish second or third generation migrant in Vienna seems to be a person who pays much attention to his or her education and integration. They are not ashamed of their origin, but they don't see their ethnical background as the universal tool of identification. They reject any comparison with other migrants who are not willing and not capable of adjusting to the society in which they live. Their parents have been struggling to raise them as successful, well-raised and well-integrated members of the Austrian society without losing their own cultural values and they want to be percieved as such.

Language – Core of the Identity Formation

Reflecting on their mother tongue, most of the interviewees were not certain how to express their attitude to the two languages in a meaningful manner. Even after the explanation that under "mother tongue" I meant "*the language which a person has grown up speaking from early childhood*" (mother tongue in The New Oxford Dictionary, 2001), they weren't sure if they should choose the language they connect to their parents and family, or the language of the society they live in. Only one of the interviewees chose German as his mother tongue without hesitation, namely because "*I think in German, not in Turkish. When I speak in Turkish, I translate in my head. (...) I can make myself understood in Turkish, but I wouldn't say that Turkish is my mother tongue*" (Richtermoc, 2014: 68). Another one claimed German as well, because she is second generation living in Austria, so it is "*self evident*". She did, with time, start to list Turkish as her mother tongue in CVs and similar documents. On the other hand, some of them claimed Turkish, mostly due to emotional reasons, even though they do not hold the same level of competency in that language.

Still, most of them chose both languages and do not feel the need or pressure in making a decision regarding the two – they chose both languages and made no difference between them. What was interesting was their decision to list Turkish as a foreign language or as their mother tongue, even though they have been confronted with common warnings to avoid listing Turkish, because it could affect their perception or employement possibilities.

Literature often regards code switching as a sign of split identities but some of the newest research shows that this situation-related switching serves as a form of regularization of social relations (Florio-Hansen & Hu, 2007:45). In the case of my communication partners, code switching mostly depended on the topic and was connected to the persons involved in the conversation. At the same time, some of the aspects of the language are never (or on the contrary, always) used in German: One of the participants claimed that she had never cursed in Turkish because it was taboo for her mother, who taught her the language. Another one said that the cultural conditioning of the Turkish language as the more passionate, more personal one, caused him to see emotionally challenging situations through a prism of the expressions of that language.

I focused heavily on the language because of its role in identity formation. In the sphere of collective identity, acquisition of a second (mother) tongue does not mean only acquisition of one extra language. It means a new membership that brings along new ways of expression, as well as different behaviours, closely linked to world ideals and moral concepts of the country of origin of that language (Florio-Hansen & Hu, 2007:89). Thanks to the bilinguality they were born into, the interviewed people felt privileged to be able to belong to both cultural circles, inheriting values and concepts of life in both spheres into their own, making themselves more able to adapt and to understand others.

Identity or the multilayered affiliation

The subjectivist attitude towards identity is closely connected to the question concerning freedom of choice, since every person is completely free in their choice of personal identification (Kalanj, 2008:46). Anthony Smith also confirms this theory that every person chooses for him or herself their belonging to an ethnical group, since it is a question of attitude, perception and sentiment, while at the same time evanescent and versatile. With changing situations, also changes of identification with a language or the meaning of these identities and their discourses for the subject might also change (Smith, 1998 in: Kalanj, 2008:46).

The respondents admitted having different phases in their claims to form (or to understand) their own identities, either as two completely different aspects of their personality, or as one identity shaped from two diverse materials. Escape from one or another identity was not percieved as a functional, nor as a manageable solution. What happened was formation of one space where one would fit; a construction of one's unique identity that would combine their partial identities, without being forced to choose between them. The phrase "*taking the best of both worlds*", often mentioned in the interviews, emerges out of their need to find another way, a third way.

They all saw their biculturality as a positive feature, one of them having said: "*That is the cleverest thing you can do with the thing you have – I gained two languages, good upringing and human warmth. (...) That is, in the end, the effect of the way I define my identity – you are, what you CAN*" (Richtermoc, 2014:75). On the other hand, most of them tried to explain that people with migration backgrounds tend to give priority to their ethnical identity when asked to choose between the two. Even though they offered similar answers to the question to which identity they felt strongly attached to, their answers did show certain inconsistencies: they have a strong emotional connection to the Turkish side, but they do not feel like they completely belong to that cultural circle (especially female respondents, who doubt the level of their rights and possibilities in Turkey). At the same time they feel that the Austrian society does not see them either as Austrians, or as migrants with backgrounds from other EU countries. That socially accepted level of discrimination goes so far, that some of them even changed their names in order to be more easily employed in the state sector, but have also carefully chosen another Turkish name that, when shortened, sounds like a typical German name.

The answers obtained prove that the young, educated second and third generation migrants mostly see their ethnical affiliation like in Bhabha's concept of hybridity of culture (where the pluricentrical modern societies enable emergence of brand new collective identifications), rather than as a discrepancy in one single identity.

My interviews proved the clear existence of the syncretic identity in the case of people with migration backgrounds. All of the sampled people affirmed their belonging to both societies, after struggling with insecurities about their identity in different phases of their youth, either in the form of denial, shame or just ignoring the existence of another identity other than an Austrian identity. It is now clear to them that they use their identities functionally and situationally. Their Austrian identity comes partly as a matter of course and partly as a result of their parents' struggles and efforts, while the Turkish one presents an additional possibility of identification that offers them a broader range of ethno-cultural features and mindset qualities. They are free to choose and pick between them, combine them and become enriched and more open-minded people.

Mutual acceptance v.s. polarized society

While analysing the interviews, I used Bremer's concept of "normative integration", meaning that the mere identification with the Republic of Austria is less important than a person's orientation and internalisation of the socially relevant norms and rules (Bertsch, 2010:22; according to Bremer, 2000:27). All of the interviewed people emphasized socially accepted norms, such as good knowledge of the language, openness to new customs and social practices, political and religious flexibility, economical independence and security, as well as moderation in keeping the ethno-cultural traditions. They reject forced assimilation and warn Austrian public not to expect only them to adapt to the society that they were born into, but also to start forming the society of variety, that fully includes members with a migration background and with no double standards for different backgrounds.

It is important to point out that precisely those who defined themselves as Austrians with Turkish migration backgrounds blame Austrian politics for the unsuccessful integration process. They believe that the Austrian society is deliberately holding the glass ceiling between the ethnical minorities and the Austrian majority in business spheres, without paying attention to second and third generation migrants at all. Namely, one of them claims that the negative image of the person with Turkish roots is perpetuated by the media and statistical data through biased portraying of first generation migrants who have troubles adjusting to the new society, and ignoring the highly educated and working class that is, according to the statistics of the Austrian Fund for Integration, almost fully equal to the population of the same profile without the migration background. On the other hand, they are aware that they represent a positive example among thousands of others who are not interested in implementing new behaviours into their own, while seeing the country of migration as the only actor in the integration process. Integration is possible only in coexistance with mutual acceptance, meaning the only way it can function, is that it goes in both directions.

My interviews have not supported the assumptions about the growing trend of re-traditionalisation between second and third generation young migrants. Instead, they see religion as a personal issue, mostly respected because of cultural tradition or older members of their families, and Turkey merely as a vacation destination, considering their knowledge of this country is based on their holiday stays there. They feel comfortable while in Turkey and do not negate the possibility of business opportunities there, but do not think about remigration due to the mere ethnical background.

I find these results important as an argument against everpresent expectations partly of the Austrian public that people with migration backgrounds, regardless of their full citizenship for generations, will eventually return back to their countries of origin. This attitude leads to one specific form of integration policy in the country, which does not include members of the second, third and further generations of migrants. Polarizing the society into the well-integrated, educated young people and the ones who are living in conservative, patriarchal families and longing for their country of origin, Austria will never be able to call itself a functioning multicultural society. The aspirations of the ones trying to find their own identity could endanger the integration process of the ones who are not as lucky to have the posibility to be raised in open minded families which have found the way to incorporate their own cultural inheritance with the country of migration, different than what their children and grandchildren were born into.

Concluding remarks: Realization of one's own identity is a way towards successful integration

The participants interviewed for this paper support the presumption that members of second and third generation citizens with Turkish migration background in Vienna are aware of their identity, whereas they question their affiliation since their early age. They do not perceive their multidimensional identities as something negative, on the contrary - through their way of life they try to find the way to adequately incorporate all these aspects into one personal identity. The feeling of double belonging that arises despite the feeling of discrepancy in some phases of their lives is not seen as a destroying element, but as an enrichment in comparison to other members of society. Through the help of their families and broadening the knowledge about their country of origin, they concluded that belonging to two different cultures represents the privilege to choose the building bricks for their personal developement. These interviews also support the claim that the concept of integration, which brings down all people with migration backgrounds to the common denominator, often calls for assimilation and is not functional as a concept in new multicultural societies such as the Austrian society.

The results of my case study show that the combination of integration and keeeping one's own ethno-cultural attributes is not impossible, it represents no threat whatsoever for the sustainability and further development of the Austrian society, but on the contrary: the circumstances that allow the developement of multiple, interpenetrating identities are the right way to form a society that values its differences.

Chapter 9: Segmentation or assimilation over the life course? Career mobility of second generation Turkish women in Germany

Jörg Hartmann

Introduction

In Germany, the second-generation migrants' share of the overall population is growing fast and, among them, those of Turkish origin represent the largest group. They are also the group with the lowest labour market outcomes, and this holds especially true for second-generation Turkish women. Of all the ethnic groups, their employment rate and hourly income are the lowest (Algan et al., 2010; Seibert, 2011), while their chances of attaining non-manual employment positions do not differ from those of native-born German women (Seibert, 2011). In addition, they have a higher risk of unemployment and being a housewife (Fincke 2009; Haug 2002), and they have the highest out of labour force rate (Luthra 2013). In comparison, other second-generation women in Germany of Iberian, Greek, or Yugoslavian origin, have less pronounced disadvantages (Heath et al. 2008). While the disadvantages of second-generation Turkish women have also been found for the Netherlands, Belgium, and Austria (Heath et al. 2008), nothing is known about the development of these disadvantages over the course of their employment careers.

There are strong reasons to study the development of ethnic inequalities over the course of the employment career. Firstly, scholars of ethnic studies need to know whether ethnic inequalities grow or decline over the course of the employment career. After all, growing ethnic labour market disadvantages over the course of the career can lead to permanent ethnic segmentation and counteract ethnic assimilation progress over the course of generations. Secondly, insights into career mechanisms of ethnic labour market disadvantages are important for policy measures that attempt to target ethnic inequalities.

As its migrant population is constantly growing, such policies will be of crucial importance for Germany. In this paper, I address the issue of second-generation Turkish women's labour market careers by comparing their income, socioeconomic status and employment opportunities to those of native-born German women. More precisely, I ask the following questions: (1) Do second-generation Turkish women have greater unemployment, greater downward income mobility and greater downward socioeconomic status mobility risks than do native-born German women? (2) Do second generation Turkish women have higher employment chances, and greater upward income mobility opportunities and greater upward socioeconomic status mobility opportunities than do native-born German women? Furthermore, I will examine the causes of any such disadvantages.

Arguments

Empirical evidence suggests that the second generation's labour market disadvantages are largely a result of their lower educational attainment (Algan et al., 2010; Granato, 2003; Kalter & Granato, 2002). Such authors argue that employment chances, income and socioeconomic status depend on individual productivity, with better education being its main determinant. Because of their greater productivity, the better educated have a competitive advantage and are more likely to be promoted (Becker, 1975; Mincer, 1974). In addition to its effect on productivity, better education increases the chances for employment in labour market segments with relatively stable positions, better protection against outside competitors and greater upward mobility. In contrast, little or no education increases the risk of entering the labour market segments with little job security and low mobility opportunities (Sengenberger, 1987). For second-generation women, I expect these risks to be greater than for native-born German women, because their educational qualifications and chances for vocational training are generally lower (Autorengruppe Bildungsberichterstattung, 2010; Kristen & Granato, 2007).

Social contacts provide information and influence, and thereby enhance career success (Granovetter, 1973). For migrants, this holds especially true for contacts that bridge ethnic groups (Kanas et al., 2012; Lancee, 2012), while social contacts within their own ethnic groups has little or no effect on labour market outcomes (Battu, Seaman, & Zenou, 2011). In support of this argument, Kalter (2006) found that second-generation male Turks employment disadvantages are indeed partly caused by their missing social contacts to the majority population. In Germany, second generation Turkish women have limited contact with native-born Germans and, for this reason, I expect their unemployment risks to be greater and their income and socioeconomic status mobility opportunities to be lower than those of native-born German women (Haug, 2003).

Events of family formation strongly shape women's employment careers. According to household economics, spouses, in their attempt to maximise family productivity, specialise in either market labour or household activity (Becker, 1981). According to this view, women, who often have lower levels of education than do their husbands, leave the labour market, especially after childbirth with its time-consuming and cost-effective consequences. In Western Germany, childbirth and marriage have been found to reduce women's labour market participation (Drobnic, Blossfeld, & Rohwer 1999; Gangl & Ziefle, 2009). In addition, studies on German second-generation migrant women found that marriage increases their employment risks (Höhne & Koopmans, 2010; Milewski, 2013). Because second generation Turkish women marry earlier in life and have more children (Milewski, 2011; Soehl & Yahirun, 2011), I expect their employment, income and socioeconomic status chances to be negatively affected by their family planning choices.

Besides the above considerations, labour market careers can produce disadvantages on their own terms. Because each employment position provides the resources of income, status, experience and contacts that can be invested into future career success, small initial disadvantages can easily restrain future career advancement. Indeed, labour market careers can be considered to be those that DiPrete and Eirich (2006) call the path-dependent form of cumulative advantages. Examples are manifold. Unemployment episodes lower the stock of human capital, send negative signals to employers and cause income losses and downward mobility (Gangl, 2006). Furthermore, initial labour market disadvantages strongly and irreversibly affects the future career (Blossfeld, 1985), while longer employment spells within the same firm increase firm-specific knowledge (Doeringer & Piore 1971). In addition, a greater number of previous jobs increases downward mobility risks (Grunow, Hofmeister & Buchholz, 2006). Given that second-generation Turkish women's employment and income chances are low (Algan et al., 2010; Seibert, 2011), and that their unemployment risks are higher (Höhne & Koopmans, 2010), the aforementioned mechanisms should restrict their upward mobility chances and increase their downward mobility risks.

In what follows, I will test whether second-generation Turkish women's lower educational qualifications, their lower share of native-born German friends, their earlier marriage and childbirth negatively affect their employment chances, unemployment risks, as well as their income and socioeconomic status mobility chances, and whether their initial disadvantages cumulate over the course of their career.

Data and methodology

In this study, I used the German Socioeconomic Panel with data from 1984 to 2010. This dataset offers monthly employment data and has the additional advantage of oversampling the German immigrant population. Due to data limitations, the sample is restricted to women aged between 18 and 35. Respondents living in East Germany were excluded, because economic and living conditions vary considerably between East and West Germany and the proportion of migrants in East Germany is negligible. Furthermore, limited case numbers only allow for three categories of ethnic origin: Native-born German women, second-generation Turkish women, and a residual category of second-generation non-Turkish women that comprise the daughters of former labour migrants from Spain, Italy, Ex-Yugoslavia and Greece. Respondents are considered to be second-generation if they migrated to Germany before the age of six or if they were born in Germany, if one of their parents migrated to Germany, and if the migrated parent has a foreign nationality or place of birth. Altogether, the sample includes 3,628 native-born German women, 247 women of Turkish origin, and 392 women of non-Turkish origin.

Career disadvantages are measured using three indicators: socioeconomic status (ISEI), gross hourly income and employment status. The ISEI index ranks occupations according to education and income, and can be understood as a measure of human resources, as well as of their economic rewards (Ganzeboom et al., 1992). Gross hourly income was chosen because working hours vary considerably among women and because net income also reflects partnership status due to the German tax principle of splitting the income taxation of married couples. Employment status is divided into three categories: Employment, unemployment and other activities unrelated to the labour market.

In order to study mobility opportunities, I applied competing risk survival analysis techniques and analysed the following transitions: (1) Upward socioeconomic status moves (2) Downward socioeconomic status moves (3) Upward income moves (4) Downward income moves (5) Moves from employment to unemployment (6) Moves from unemployment to employment. These upward and downward transitions not only provide a comprehensive picture of labour market related mobility disadvantages, but their joint balance also depicts the growth or decrease of ethnic inequalities over the employment career. For occupational and income moves, the process time is defined as the duration in a certain job until a 10 per cent change in either socioeconomic status (ISEI) or gross hourly income occurs. While the 10 per cent threshold is somewhat arbitrary, it is designed to cover a substantial change in income and socioeconomic status. For employment moves, the time axis starts whenever a change in employment status occurs and ends with a further change in the employment status. Respondents whose first job is not reported in the dataset are excluded so as to avoid left censoring. In addition, transitions into self-employment are treated as right-censored and are excluded, because income and socioeconomic status variation within self-employment episodes does not yield any substantial meaning.

In line with the hypotheses, I included a number of independent variables in the models. The age and labour market entry cohorts are included in order to account for historical macro-economic conditions at labour market entry and life cycle effects. Educational attainment is included and is operationalised according to the CASMIN scheme. Furthermore, I included the number of native-born German friends among the three best friends to measure the social integration into the majority population. In addition, events of family formation are measured by monthly marriage status and the number of children, and I split those episodes that overlapped with employment episodes. The firm's size and a dummy variable for employment in the public sector are used to measure the labour market sector. The public sector is a prime example of an internal labour market with stable positions and well-defined upward trajectories, while internal labour markets outside the public sector are more likely to be found in larger firms. Finally, the employment history is measured using the months of previous unemployment, months of work experience, the number of job changes and the first income and status.

Results

Do second-generation women experience socioeconomic status, income, and employment mobility disadvantages? Table 9.1 presents the effects of belonging to the second generation Turkish and non-Turkish groups on the transition rate, compared to native-born German women. For each transition (tables A. to F.), the first model (M1) only displays the effects of ethnic group membership, while the second model (M2) displays the effects of ethnic group membership for people of the same age and labour market entry cohort. Because income and socioeconomic status mobility vary for different levels of income and socioeconomic status, I attained fully comparable effects for income and socioeconomic status transition by including the current income and socioeconomic status for the respective transitions (tables C. to F., model M3).

Most notably, second generation Turkish women have greater unemployment risks (B. M2), as well as greater income and socioeconomic status downward mobility risks than do native-born German women (D., F. M3). Also, their unemployment, income and downward mobility risks are greater than are those of average, non-Turkish second-generation women. Moreover, the results indicate that the second-generation Turkish women's greater downward risks are not compensated for by greater upward mobility chances. Their chances of re-entering employment (A. M2) and their opportunities for upward income and socioeconomic status mobility (C., E. M3) equal those of native-born German women. The second-generation Turkish women's upward mobility chances are also below those of the average non-Turkish second-generation women. As a result, the employment, income, and socioeconomic status gaps widen between second-generation Turkish women and native-born German women over the course of the career.

When attempting to explain these disadvantages, I first introduced educational attainment into the models. With education held constant in table B., model M3, second generation Turkish women's greater unemployment risks are reduced to 0,106 and are insignificant. The same applies to second-generation women's greater downward income mobility risks: when education is held constant, their greater downward income mobility risks decrease from 0,346 (table D., M3) to 0,161 (table D., M4). Likewise, second-generation Turkish women's greater downward socioeconomic mobility risks are reduced from 0,556 (table F., model M3) to 0,388 (table F., model M4) when the educational level is held constant, even though their disadvantages remain significant.

Therefore, I introduced the number of their German friends (M5), their timing of marriage and childbirth (M6), the firm's size and the public sector (M7) and measures for their more disadvantaged previous employment history (M8), in addition to the education level. As the results reveal, the downward socioeconomic status mobility disadvantages of second-generation Turkish women decrease to insignificant 0,265 (table F., model M5) when, in addition to their lower education, their percentage of German friends is taken into account. Among the other variables added to education, only the previous labour market career reduces the second-generation Turkish women's disadvantages somewhat. However, model M5 is the only model that reduces second-generation Turkish women's greater socioeconomic status downward mobility risks to insignificant levels and all other hypotheses mus be rejected.

Table 9.1. Coefficients for ethnic origin, using competing risks Cox proportional hazards models

A. Unempl. to Empl.	Turks		Others		Log Lik
M1: Origin	0,251		0,111		-4611,7
M2: M1 + Age + Cohort	0,215		0,082		-4607,7
M3: M2 + Education	0,045		0,015		-4588,3
M4: M3 + Friends	0,093		-0,034		-4582,9
M5: M3 + Family	0,154		0,068		-4528,9
M6: M3 + Sector + Size	-0,161		-0,030		-4204,4
M7: M3 + Emp. history	-0,155		-0,166		-4284,2
M8: all	0,237		0,043		-3881,2
B. Emp. to Unempl.	**Turks**		**Others**		Log Lik
M1: Origin	0,469	***	0,011		-9685,8
M2: M1 + Age + Cohort	0,451	***	-0,004		-9668,7
M3: M2 + Education	0,106		-0,213		-9439,3
M4: M3 + Friends	-0,032		-0,339	*	-9432,1
M5: M3 + Family	0,228		0,197		-9416,7
M6: M3 + Sector + Size	0,111		-0,208		-9317,8
M7: M3 + Emp. history	0,059		-0,228	*	-9230,2
M8: all	-0,057		-0,313	*	-9155,1
C. Income Upward Mobility	**Turks**		**Others**		Log Lik
M1: Origin	-0,029		0,138	*	-12457,6
M2: M1 + Age + Cohort	-0,036		0,138	*	-12444,1
M3: M2 + Income	-0,074		0,146	*	-12325,4
M4: M3 + Education	0,065		0,209	**	-12266,9
M5: M4 + Friends	0,156		0,265	**	-12263,1
M6: M4 + Family	-0,001		0,203	**	-12257,3

	Turks		Others		Log Lik
M7: M4 + Sector + Size	0,067		0,214	**	-12215,4
M8: M4 + Emp. history	0,062		0,237	**	-12240,2
M9: all	0,111		0,309	***	-12187,0
D. Income Downward Mobility	**Turks**		**Others**		Log Lik
M1: Origin	0,335		0,319	*	-2825,1
M2: M1 + Age + Cohort	0,346		0,329	*	-2821,6
M3: M2 + Income	0,372	*	0,328	*	-2814,5
M4: M3 + Education	0,161		0,207		-2796,8
M5: M4 + Friends	0,141		0,206		-2796,4
M6: M4 + Family	0,276		0,217		-2790,1
M7: M4 + Sector + Size	0,167		0,194		-2791,0
M8: M4 + Emp. history	0,207		0,219		-2793,7
M9: all	0,371		0,213		-2780,7
E. ISEI Upward Mobility	**Turks**		**Others**		Log Lik
M1: Origin	0,133		0,272		-6761,5
M2: M1 + Age + Cohort	0,165		0,300	***	-6753,7
M3: M2 + ISEI	-0,104		0,221	*	-6612,9
M4: M3 + Education	0,037		0,292	**	-6551,6
M5: M4 + Friends	0,131		0,347	**	-6549,6
M6: M4 + Family	0,034		0,291	**	-6551,2
M7: M4 + Sector + Size	0,006		0,279	**	-6527,3
M8: M4 + Emp. history	-0,016		0,324	***	-6521,4
M9: all	0,083		0,346	***	-6496,8
F. ISEI Downward Mobility	**Turks**		**Others**		Log Lik
M1: Origin	0,264	*	0,271	**	-5455,0
M2: M1 + Age + Cohort	0,324	**	0,326	**	-5447,2
M3: M2 + ISEI	0,556	***	0,433	***	-5389,2
M4: M3 + Education	0,388	**	0,342	**	-5327,3
M5: M4 + Friends	0,265		0,308	*	-5325,6
M6: M4 + Family	0,376	**	0,344	**	-5326,4

M7: M4 + Sector + Size	0,385 **	0,341 **	-5320,8
M8: M4 + Emp. history	0,301 *	0,310 **	-5300,2
M9: all	0,249	0,282 *	-5290,6

Discussion and conclusion

Looking at employment, income, and socioeconomic status risks and chances of second-generation Turkish women in Germany, this study reveals that they have higher unemployment risks and higher risks of income and socioeconomic status downward mobility over the course of their early employment career. At the same time, their re-employment and income or socioeconomic status upward mobility chances do not significantly differ, indicating that their employment, income, and socioeconomic status disadvantages grow as they get older. As for their greater unemployment and income downward mobility risks, the results show that both are a result of their lower educational attainment. In addition, the results show that their higher socioeconomic status downward mobility risks can be fully explained by a combination of their lower educational level and their missing social contacts to the majority population.

This study adds to the existing literature in three main ways: Firstly, this study adds a longitudinal perspective to second-generation Turkish women's employment disadvantages, contributing to the important insight of their greater employment, income, and socioeconomic mobility risks over the course of their early labour market career. Secondly, this study confirms previous findings on the role of educational attainment and bridging social contacts to the majority population for the labour market success of second-generation migrants (Kalter & Granato, 2002; Kalter, 2006). Thirdly, this study challenges findings that events of family formation, labour market sector, or the previous employment career have significant effects of second-generation migant's labour market career (cp. Höhne & Koopmans, 2010).

In the light of these findings, second-generation Turkish women seem to be in a particularly disadvantaged position in German society.

Even though we know that their labour market outcomes have improved compared to their mothers (Milewski, 2013), their higher employment, income, and socioeconomic status risks over the course of their career give rise to concerns about their overall assimilation progress. Given the rather close link between the occupational positions of parents and their children in Germany (Müller & Pollak, 2004) the effects of intragenerational assimilation should not be underestimated.

While this study aimed at assessing second-generation Turkish women's mobility risks and chances, further research is necessary to fully understand their distinctive disadvantages in the German labour market. Most importantly, their labour market trajectories need to be studied using panel data models. Such studies should also include alternative positions not looked at in this study, namely household activities. In addition, the role of gender role values, cultural values, and partner characteristics for second-generation Turkish women's labour market disadvantages has only been studied recently and needs to be addressed in further longitudinal studies (Köbrich, 2013; Höhne & de Valk 2010).

From a policy perspective, the results emphasise the need for labour market policies that are targeted directly at decreasing the employment, income and socioeconomic status gap between second generation Turkish and native-born German women. As the gap in employment, income and socioeconomic status increases and is likely to be passed on to the third generation, policies that help to reduce the gap will not only benefit the second Turkish generation directly, but also their children. Most importantly, this study underlines that the importance of parity in educational opportunities cannot be overstressed. Policy makers therefore have strong leverage to enhance the future prospects of second-generation Turkish women in Germany.

Chapter 10: How highly skilled labour migrants deal with flexibility?

Ulaş Sunata

During the last three decades, the phenomenon of flexibility has attracted a great deal of attention in sociology, not only in relation to work flexibility but also flexibility of migration. In this respect, the structural changes in both employment relationships and migratory conditions have brought about new lifestyles. The theoretical debates in the field of migration studies and human capital have often concentrated on the (changing) roles of nation-states, transnational corporations, and recruitment agencies at the macro level. Sassen (1988; 1998) observed two critical social classes and their spatial polarization in transnational migration. *P*eople from low income groups are employed in low-skilled service jobs. *In contrast*, there are newly emerging high income segments employed in professions. Th*is* latter group are also the *"young urban professionals"* (yuppies) who tend to be portrayed as enjoying affluent lifestyles (Robinson, 2009). In other words, they are referred to as the *"role-model"* group for flexible life. For them, this means frofessional job autonomy, team working experience led by projects, flexible working hours, part-time work, term-time working, home-based teleworking, time off in lieu, sabbaticals and career breaks that are usually presented as employee-friendly flexibility features (Fleetwood, 2007; Peters, Den Hulk, & van der Lippe, 2009). However, flexibility friendliness should be questioned if the employee is a migrant at the same time, or in the process of becoming a migrant for the purpose of work. This chapter deals with the micro level question of how professionals or skilled workers who work in a country other than that of their country of birth integrate into this new lifestyle of flexible working.

There are various definitions of "flexibility" (i.e. labour market flexibility). According to Atkinson (1984), there are four kinds of labour market flexibilities: (i) external numerical flexibility (temporary or fixed-term employment contracts), (ii) internal numerical flexibility (overtime, part-time work and irregular working times; working time flexibility), (iii) functional flexibility (task and job rotation, outsourcing), and (iv) wage flexibility. The *first* two *of these* (*external and internal* numerical flexibility) highlight temporal flexibility, which highlights the issues of employment protection and working time. In addition, Reilly (2001) and Wallace (2003) mention spatial flexibility, which is linked to the labour practices regardless of where you work. Flexibility usually implies contract-based workwhile project deadlines and meeting with customers or co-workers determining temporal flexibility and commuting between different work places refers to spatial flexibility (Sunata, 2011, p.257).[1]

In the literature, temporal-spatial flexibility is inextricably associated with work-life balance (Nyström, 2005; Fleetwood, 2007; König & Cesinger, 2015) since the flexibility has been stated to work well with the modern family types and is well received in the business world. However, it is possible to state that it changes work and home situations. With changing family compositions, Bellavia and Frone (2005) stress the increasing importance of the work-family conflict during recent decades. Most proposed solutions call for flexible labour conditions (Allen, 2001). As a matter of fact, men and women express both increased job-related stress and a desire for work flexibility (Allen, 2008; Kerpelman & Schvaneveldt, 1999). Current studies suggest that time-spatial flexible work provides for the reconciliation of work and family life (Nyström, 2005; König & Cesinger, 2015) while creating *"discontinuity of social relations at the workplace"* (Nyström, 2005, p.24). A current study however shows men's reluctance to seek work flexibility due to fears of gender-related stigmatization (Vandello, Hettinger, Bosson, & Siddiqi, 2013). It suggests the importance of pressures to conform to traditional gender roles on employees. Besides these clear indications for the persistence

---

[1] Sunata (2011, p.257) hence suggests this is better termed variability rather than flexibility.

of the gendered picture, the lack of significant gender differences regarding work flexibility still indicate a shift (König & Cesinger, 2015).

A consequence of flexible working conditions is the absence of a lifelong job guarantee, the lack of labour union membership, project-based work, working with transitional colleagues, and uncertain shift start and end times. They depend on such developments in the labour market as fee-charging from the recruitment process and the change of typical employment relationships. Indeed, employment relations are no longer only bilateral and of a definite nature but also "triangular" between each duality of the private employment agency, the employer, and the employee, and mostly it is of an indefinite nature (Sunata, 2011, pp.203-209). With a diminishing of routine and increased risk in continuity of working for employees in labour relations, all these destroy the old work ethic and hamper solidarity. Instead, the emergence of life-long learning and a new form of communicative skills for professional adaptation to every new work situation shape the new work culture. For the highly-educated migrants, flexibility implies working in an international atmosphere, speaking predominantly English, and exhibiting cultural plurality of work habits. It is worth noting that contract-based work demands a flexible lifestyle and preparedness. On the one hand, temporal flexibility decomposes working time, blurs work-time boundaries, and creates an illusion about plenty of recreation time. Spatial flexibility, on the other hand, seems to be valid for the workplace, but alters the worker's home setting while blurringthe spatial boundaries between family and work.

Fleetwood (2007) determines practices of employer-friendly or employee-unfriendly flexibility as involuntary temporary working, involuntary part-time working, temporal labour contracts, unsocial working atmosphere, and unpredictable working hours. In this study, we will question the friendliness of temporal-spatial flexibility. Temporal dimension of flexibility is operationalized by employment protection and working time by helping Atkinson's concept of numerical flexibility (1984). Its spatial dimension is also questioned. It should be underlined that the discourses on employee-friendly flexibility do not necessarily reflect the practices (Fleetwood, 2007).

Harvey (2005) and Fleetwood (2007) interpret flexibility discourse with neoliberalism: "*a new class strategy whereby the iron fist of a renewed ruling class offensive is wrapped in the velvet glove of freedom, individualism and, above all, flexibility*" (Fleetwood, 2007, p.388; emphasis is mine).

Sunata (2011, p.260) presents a threefold typology of highly-skilled labour migrants' approach to work that is defined as the degree of integration in the flexible labour market, following unitary, flexible, and critical integration. The author emphasizes that a clear majority of highly educated migrant workers identify themselves by their capability to integrate into the flexible labour conditions. The flexibly integrated type tend to be aware of the change in work relations and tries to adapt by accepting a variable lifestyle oriented around work. They take risks in an attempt to find secure working conditions. The market offers them various job opportunities, based on the companies with which the migrants are affiliated, but only until a certain age after which opportunities are scarce. However, they consider themselves impotent to influence these labour relations.

This chapter focuses on the ways in which Turkish highly-skilled migrants deal with flexible work conditions in Germany. It examines the flexible geography of highly skilled labour migration through a case study from the life course perspective. Based on purposively selected in-depth interviews with internationally-mobile engineers from Turkey in Germany, it explores the time-specific meanings attached to migrants' labour market relations, and their positions in negotiating the flexible patterns of labour relations in their migration experiences. Through migratory history, working biographical information and self-evaluations, the study will examine (i) how highly-skilled workers negotiate changes in working and migratory conditions over time and (ii) what kind of similarities and differences there are in their situations as time goes on. In fact, the analysis will attempt to understand not only cross-section views of their social background but also their concrete experiences to handle flexibility. Consequently, it will reveal information about continued structural transformation in terms of the labour market and migration provoked by flexibility across the last three decades. Furthermore, it will indicate that the main agents' longitudinal strategies correlate with the individual life period.

Method

Qualitative methods were favoured to understand migratory experiences in a flexible labour market and attempt to develop a contextually relevant quantitative measure, based on qualitative data. Between 2005 and 2006, I conducted a comprehensive qualitative study about highly skilled labour migration from Turkey to Germany. The study built a database of 123 Turkish ICT-Specialists who have at least one year working experience in Germany in the decade of 1995-2005. This database of Turkish highly-skilled labour migration in the German context also covers 66 semi-structured interviews. For this study, I reconsidered a sub group of 33 interviews from the database.

Table 1. Demographic Profile

	Age	Marital Status	Germany Residence	Migration Experience (circa)	Departure Date
Acer palmatum (A)	29	single	1 year	5 years	2000
Fraxinus excelsior (F)	39	single	4 years	15 years	1991
Quercus pyrenaica (Q)	47	Married(10years)	14 years	20 years	1985

I deliberately selected context-dependent extreme cases (purposive sampling) in the database. The selection criterion is to have working experience in at least three different countries except for the country of origin, as presented in Table 3. This criterion makes the sample size three out of 33, by coincidence in different age-groups, as noted in Table 1. But it was so important to explain different stages in the life course in relation to flexibility. Therefore our purposive sample consists of three internationally-mobile engineer participants. Two in-depth interviews took place in Stuttgart and one in Frankfurt.

All of the selected participants are men. The participants are originally from Turkey and work in Germany as the current country of residence at the time of the interviews. They graduated as electrical and electronic engineers from universities in Turkey. As noted in Table 1, each of them initially went abroad for work or educational purposes in 1985, 1991, and 2000, respectively. Afterwards, they have migrated to various countries for work (disregarding international business trips). Each experience in their international career path has taken at least four months.

Results

Flexibility requires Career-Orientation

The socioeconomic background of the three cases in very mobile skilled migration is strikingly similar, as seen in Table 2. The education of all but one of "housewife" mothers is limited to primary education and their fathers are graduates of, at least, secondary education. In addition, the fathers have worked as technician or low level civil servants, but currently they are retired. All three participants came from (lower-) middle class families in Turkey that valued education. All children of their families are graduated from university and working as professionals. These families sent their children to public schools and universities. More specifically, the lower middle class children are more likely to benefit from state initiatives rather than private options.

Like skilled migrants, very mobile participants did not have any family network in Germany or their other destination countries. Interviewee-2 gained graduate study experience abroad, while Interviewee-3 studied in Turkey. Relatively new migrants, Interviewee-1 and Interviewee-2, were green card holders in Germany. Interviewee-2 had double citizenship, due to owning a Canadian passport. Interviewee-3 as an old migrant had a German permanent residency permit.

Table 2. Socio-Economic Status of Family

	Educational Position		Occupational Position		Siblings' Position	
	Father	Mother	Father	Mother	Sister	Brother
A	11 years	11 years	Civil Servant (Retired)	Housewife	University Graduate	University Graduate
F	13 years	5 years	Technician (Retired)	Housewife	Teacher	Teacher
Q	11 years	5 years	Technician (Retired)	Housewife	Pharmacist	Engineer

Table 3. Working Experience

	Working Experience	*Details*
A	Turkey, the UK, Saudi Arabia, Turkey, Germany, Turkey, Germany	Head-hunter, intra-company movement, relocation, green card, international certificate exams
F	Turkey, the UK, Turkey, Canada, the US, Canada, Germany	Master degree, double citizenship, contractor firms, green card
Q	Turkey, Denmark, Turkey, Germany, Belgium, Germany	Efforts of adaptation with flexibility and difficulty of professional security

The respondents did not come to Germany directly from Turkey. The three men first left Turkey for other countries of destination, such as UK, Canada, and Denmark. They are more flexible in crossing borders as skilled labour than other cases. Moreover, they change their

131

FAMILY AND HUMAN CAPITAL IN TURKISH MIGRATION

companies whenever they move country. Germany at the time of the interview was the fourth country of working, i.e. third country of destination. Their common features are having working experience in Turkey and being well-trained for the whole international skilled labour market, not specifically for the German labour market. They are more likely to hold graduate degrees or international certificates.

The socioeconomic upward mobility (lower-to-upper-middle class) of these three participants is explicit. Moreover, they usually work for international corporations and their jobs are mostly contract-based. It is noticeable that they easily decide to move and they have clear upward career mobility through migration in their biographies, both educational and occupational careers. Furthermore, they work for international companies under more apparently flexible working conditions, and all prefer to speak English as the business language. They mostly identify themselves by their work and never make use of labour unions to consolidate their position. Based on the participants' background information it is clear that all three participants are career-oriented liberal ICT-Specialist men.

Flexibility is seen as a change in career structure

Almost all skilled workers recognize the absence of a lifelong job guarantee in the current working conditions. For instance; Interviewee-2 was working on a short-term contract basis, but the temporary nature of his job did not bother him, and he accepted that at his relatively young age. He argued that this situation was his choice, and he could have behaved differently if he had been 45 or older, preferring a more stable work life. Indeed, he prefers the temporary nature of his current job due to the associated flexibility, arguing that, thanks to his age, the probability of insecurity is irrelevant before the threshold age of 45. However, as seen in the interview with Interviewee-3, the subject with the longest foreign working experience, the insecurity of the labour relations increases over time. In fact, he underlined that flexible working implied both increased income but also increased risk in comparison to that experienced by the typical employee. The recent labour relations appear insecure and transitional, a consequence of their flexibility. As a matter of fact, they always maintain a second option in case they loose their jobs. Thus, all of them are not afraid by the possibility of losing their jobs, particularly in their young ages. They consider that this could happen and that it would not necessarily be a consequence of their failure.

Table 4. Perceptions towards Home and Job Security

	Home	**Job security**
Interviewee-1	Making money	Making money
Interviewee-2	Nowhere	Taking risk
Interviewee-3	Double/multiple	Pragmatism

As the labour migrants grow older, perception towards temporal-spatial flexibility vary. This study, on the one side, propose the change in their interpretations of home (money – nowhere – double/multiple, respectively) in the life course as an indicator of questioning the spatial dimension of flexibility. On the other, the radical alteration in old age of their perceptions towards job security (making money, taking risk, pragmatism, respectively) and their tendency to conserve marital status related with the stress on starting a family (single – single – married without child, respectively) should be taken in consideration in order to explain temporal dimension of flexibility. Delaying marriage until they have proved themselves in their career is such a coping mechanism with insecurity in the work environment since they see marriage as a form of risk. They argue that being single is a financial benefit.

Discussion and conclusion

Previous analyses of flexibility have occluded scales and processes that are critical to understanding how flexibility dynamics are linked to the spatial aspects of migration. By contrast, such focus on the flexible and time-based contexts of migration illustrates the complex interactions between migrants' temporal interpretations of flexibility and migration. When examining these interactions, flexibility can be conceptualised as ontologically inseparable from migration, rethinking temporal logic and pragmatic views of flexibility and migration put forth in the life course theory.

The study reveals findings about highly-skilled labour migrants who appear to be adapting to flexible work practices at most. The first one is the similar socio-economic backgrounds of top flexible migrants and their common upward mobility. This result warrants a thought on the difference of brain drain migration experience of (lower-) middle class children from upper-middle class children. The second finding exposes dominance of individualistic behaviour among these people. They usually promote the exercise of their goals and desires, as well as they value self-reliance and personal independence. To sum up, it can be argued that flexibility requires to have a demand for upward mobility and to be highly individualistic.

International labour migration, especially of highly educated people, is not always associated with unemployment and wage differentials, but perceived as an element of career building (Sunata, 2011, p.278). Highly skilled labour migrants experience their own working and migration experiences together and perceive as their individual freedom. Being highly individualized, the related migrants are interested in integration into the labour market for their career building, but at the same time they try to integrate into the new social environment in order to value experience abroad. Along these lines, Sunata (2011, pp.273-279) found the importance of leisure participation as means of attempts at overall their integration.

The most important finding of this study is that the participants' longitudinal strategies in order to deal with flexibility are correlated with the individual's life period. The chapter examined how highly-educated migrant workers negotiate changes in working and migratory conditions over periods and what kind of similarities and differences among their experience as time goes on. In fact, the analysis attempted to understand not only cross-section views of their social background but also their concrete experiences in handling flexibility. Consequently, this work reveals information about continued structural transformation in terms of the labour market and migration provoked by flexibility across the last three decades. Furthermore, it shows to see that the main agents' longitudinal strategies correlated with the individual life period. This study could be improved significantly through an insight into intrinsic and extrinsic motivation related to work contracts and expectations following the lines of the psychological contract.

One limitation of the present research is its lack of attention to the organizational level that contributes to how recruitment agencies, employers and unions utilize or criticize flexibility. A better understanding of the interplay of these organizational actors with workers would provide a more comprehensive account of friendliness in flexibility in practice. Another limitation of this study is the presentation of unique work flexibility in terms of degree and form. This study concentrated on high degree of flexibility of ICT sector. It causes the low explanatory power for different degree and model of flexibility.

References

Ahmed, S. (2004). *The cultural politics of emotion*. Edinburgh: Edinburgh University Press.

Algan, Y., Dustmann, C., Glitz, A., & Manning, A. (2010). The Economic Situation of First and Second-Generation Immigrants in France, Germany and the United Kingdom. *The Economic Journal, 120*(542), F4-F30.

Allen, T. D. (2001). Family-supportive work environments: The role of organizational perceptions. *Journal of vocational behavior*, 58(3), 414-435.

Allen, T. D. (2008). Integrating career development and work-family policy. Cambridge, UK: Cambridge University Press.

Allison, P. D. (1994). Using Panel Data to Estimate the Effects of Events. *Sociological Methods & Research, 23,* 174-199.

Arnold F. (1987). Birds of passage no more: Migration decision-making among Filipino immigrants in Hawaii. *International Migration*, 25(1), 41-61.

Atkinson, J. (1984). Flexibility, Uncertainty and Manpower Management. IMS Report No.89, Brighton: Institute of Manpower Studies.

Atkinson, J., & Meager, N. (1986). Changing Working Patterns: How companies achieve flexibility to meet new needs. London: Institute of Manpower Studies, National Economic Development Office.

Autorengruppe Bildungsberichterstattung (2010). *Bildung in Deutschland 2010: Ein indikatorengestützter Bericht mit einer Analyse zu Perspektiven des Bildungswesens im demografischen Wandel*. Bielefeld: Bertelsmann.

Aybek, C., Straßburger, G., &Yüksel-Kaptanoglu, I. (2015). Marriage migration from Turkey to Germany: Risks and coping strategies of transnational couples. *Aybek, C., Huinink, J., & Muttarak, R. (eds.) Spatial Mobility, Migration, and Family Dynamics.* Dordrecht: Springer, 23-42.

Baldassar, L. (2001). *Visits home: Migration experiences between Italy and Australia*. Melbourne: Melbourne University Press.

Baldassar, L. (2007). Transnational families and aged care: The mobility of care and the migrancy of ageing. *Journal of Ethnic and Migration Studies, 33*(2): 275–297.

Baldassar, L. (2008). Missing Kin and Longing to Be Together: Emotions and the Construction of Co-presence in Transnational Relationships. *Journal of Intercultural Studies*, 29(3): 247 –266.

Battu, H., Seaman, P., & Zenou Y. (2011). Job contact networks and the ethnic minorities. *Labour Economics, 18*(1), 48-56.

Baykara-Krumme, H. (2014). Three-generation marriage patterns: New insights from the 'dissimilation' perspective. *Journal of Ethnic and Migration Studies*. doi: 10.1080/1369183X.2014.980720 (online first).

Baykara-Krumme, H. (2013). Generationenbeziehungen im Alter: Türkische Familien in der Türkei und in Westeuropa (Intergenerational relationships in old age: Turkish families in Turkey and in Western Europe). *Zeitschrift für Familienforschung* (Journal of Family Research) 25(1), 9-28.

Becker, G. S. (1975). *Human Capital: A theoretical and empirical analysis, with special reference to education.* Chicago: The University of Chicago Press.

Becker, G. S. (1981). *A Treatise on the family.* Cambridge, MA: Harvard University Press.

Bell, C. (1992). *Ritual Theory. Ritual Practice*, New York, Oxford: Oxford University Press.

Bellavia, G. M., & Frone, M. R. (2005). Work-family conflict. Barling, J., Kelloway, E. K., & Frone, M. R. (Eds.) *Handbook of work stress.* Sage. pp. 113-147.

Berkhout E., Smid T., & Volkerink, M. (2010). *Wat beweegt kennismigranten? Een analyse van concurrentiekracht van Nederland bij het aantrekken van kennis-migranten.* Amsterdam: SEO Economisch Onderzoek.

Bermejo, I., Hölzel, L., Kriston, L., & Härter, M. (2012). Subjektiv erlebte Barrieren von Personen mit Migrationshintergrund bei der Inanspruchnahme von Gesundheitsmaßnahmen. [Subjectively experienced barriers of people with migration background at utilisation of health care measures.] *Bundesgesundheitsblatt, 55*(8), 944–953 (in German).

Bernhardt, E., and Goldscheider, F. (2007). Marriage and cohabitation. In E. Bernhardt, C. Goldscheider, F. Goldscheider, and G. Bjeren (Eds.): *Immigration, Gender and Family Transitions to Adulthood in Sweden* (pp. 55-72). Lanham et al.: University Press of America.

Bertsch, N. (2010). Die Situation von in zweiter und dritter Generation in Österreich lebenden ,TürkInnen' in Bezug auf Integration, Vorurteile, Diskriminierungen und Rassismus. [The situation of "Turks" of second and third generation in Austria concerning integration, prejudice, discrimination and racism] Unpublished diploma thesis. University of Vienna (in German)

Blohm, M., & Diehl, C. (2001). Wenn Migranten Migranten befragen: Zum Teilnahmever-halten von Einwanderern bei Bevölkerungsbefragungen. [When migrants question migrants: On participation behaviour of immigrants in population surveys.] *Zeitschrift für Soziologie, 30*(3), 223–242 (in German).

Blossfeld, H. P. (1985). Berufseintritt und Berufsverlauf: eine Kohortenanalyse über die Bedeutung des ersten Berufs in der Erwerbsbiographie. *Mitteilungen aus der Arbeitsmarkt-und Berufsforschung, 18*(2), 177-197.

Bosma, H., Jackson, S., Zijsling, D., Zani, B., Cicognani, E., Lucia X., et al. (1996).Who has the final say? Decisions on adolescent behaviour within the family.*Journal of Adolescence,* 19(3), 277-291.

Brah, A. (1996). *Cartographies of diaspora: Contesting Identities.* London: Routledge.

Brown, S.K. and Bean, F.D. (2006). International migration. In: *Handbook of Population*, D.L. Poston and M. Micklin (eds.). Springer: Texas, pp. 347-382.

Bryceson, D. & Vuorela, U. (2002). *The Transnational Family: Global European Networks and New Frontiers.* Oxford, New York: Berg.

Burkitt, Ian (2002). Complex Emotions: Relations, Feelings and Images in Emotional Experience. In: Barbalet, J. (ed.) *Emotions and Sociology*, Oxford and Malden: Blackwell Publishing, pp 151–167.

Buunk, A.P., Park, J.H. & Duncan, L.A. (2010).Cultural variation in parental influence on mate choice.*Cross-Cultural Research*, 44(1), 23-40.

Carnein, M.; Milewski, N.; Doblhammer, G.; Nusselder, W.J. (2015). Health inequalities of immigrants: Patterns and determinants of health expectancies of Turkish migrants living in Germany. In: Doblhammer, G. (Ed.): Health among the elderly in Germany: New evidence on disease, disability and care need. Series on Population Studies by the Federal Institute for Population Research, Vol. 46, Opladen, Berlin, Toronto: Barbara Budrich, 157-190.

Carol, S. (2014). The intergenerational transmission of intermarriage attitudes and intergroup friendships: The role of Turkish migrant parents. *Journal of Ethnic and Migration Studies*, 40(10), 1550-1571.

Celikaksoy, A., Nekby, L. & Rashid, S.(2010). Assortative mating by ethnic background and education among individuals with an immigrant background in Sweden.*ZeitschriftfürFamilienforschung/Journal of Family Research*, 22(1), 65-88.

Chamberlain, M. & Leydesdorff, S. (2004). Transnational families: Memories and narratives. *Global Networks*, 4(3): 227–241.

Chiswick, B. R. & Miller, P. W. (1995). The Endogeneity between Language and Earnings: International Analyses. *Journal of labor economics, 13,* 246-288.

Chotkowski, M., Liu, J. & Nicolaas, H. Gezinsmigratie (2014). Gezinsmigratie. In R.P.W. Jennissen & H. Nicholaas (eds.). *De Nederlandse Migratiekaart 2013. Achtergronden en ontwikkelingen in internationale migratiestromen in de periode vanaf 2000.* Cahier 2014-8. Den Haag: WODC/CBS, p. 69-96.

Cohen, J., and Sirkeci, I. (2011). *Cultures of Migration, the Global Nature of Contemporary Mobility*, University of Texas Press, Austin, USA.

Crul, M., Schneider, J. & Lelie, F., eds. (2012). *The European second generation compared. Does the integration context matter?* Amsterdam, Chicago: Amsterdam University Press.

Currie, J. & Thomas, D. (1995). Does Head Start Make a Difference? *The American Economic Review, 85,* 341-364.

Czernomoriez, J. (2009). Internationale Wanderungen von Humankapital und wirtschaftliches Wachstum. *Volkswirtschaftliche Schriften, 557.* Diss. Duncker & Humblot, Universität Potsdam.

De Florio-Hansen, I., Hu, A. (2008). Plurilingualität und Identität. Zur Selbst-und Fremdwahrnehmung mersprachiger Menschen. [Multilingualism and Identity]. Tübingen, Stauffenberg Verlag (in German)

De Valk, H. A. G. & Liefbroer, A.C. (2007). Timing preferences for women's family-life transitions: Intergenerational transmission among migrants and Dutch. *Journal of Marriage and Family, 69*(1), 190-206.

Dessing, N. (2001). *Rituals of Birth, Circumcision, Marriage and Death among Muslims in the Netherlands.* Leuven: Peeters.

Diehl, C. & Schnell, R. (2006). "Reactive Ethnicity" or "Assimilation"? Statement, Arguments, and First Empirical Evidence for Labor Migrants in Germany. *International Migration Review, 40,* 786-816.

DiPrete, T. A., & Eirich, G. M. (2006). Cumulative advantage as a mechanism for inequality: A review of theoretical and empirical developments. *Annual Review of Sociology, 32,* 271-297.

Downer, J. T. & Pianta, R. C. (2006). Academic and cognitive Functioning in first grade: Associations with earlier Home and Child Care Predictors and with Concurrent Home and Classroom Experiences. *School Psychology Review, 35,* 11-30.

Drobnic, S., Blossfeld, H.-P., & Rohwer, G. (1999). Dynamics of women's employment patterns over the family life course: A comparison of the United States and Germany. *Journal of Marriage and the Family, 61*(1), 133-146.

Ellis, C. & Bochner, A.P. (2000). Auto-ethnography, personal narrative, reflexivity: researcher as subject notes*, Denzin, N. and Y. Lincoln, Y. (eds.) The Handbook Of Qualitative Research, Thousand Oaks, Sage, California, pp. 733-768.*

Esser, H. (1980): *Aspekte der Wanderungssoziologie.* Darmstadt, Neuwied: Luchterhand.

European Parliament (2010). *The Lisbon Strategy 2000-2010: An analysis of the methods used and results achieved. Final Report. Directorate General for Internal Policies, Policy Department A: Economic and Scientific Policy, Employment and Social Affairs.* Brussels: European Parliament.

Federal Employment Agency (FEA) (2011). *Perspektive 2025: Fachkräfte für Deutschland.* Nürnberg.

Federal Ministry of Labour and Social Affairs (Bundesministerium für Arbeit und Soziales (BMAS)) (2011). *Fachkräftesicherung.* Ziele und Maßnahmen der Bundesregierung. Berlin.

Federal Office for Migration and Refugees (BAMF) (2013). *Migrationsbericht.* Migrationsbericht des Bundesamtes für Migration und Flüchtlinge im Auftrag der Bundesregierung. Migrationsbericht 2012. Nürnberg.

Federal Office for Migration and Refugees (Bundesamt für Migration und Flüchtlinge (BAMF)) (2004). *Migrationsbericht.* Migrationsbericht des Bundesamtes für Migration und Flüchtlinge im Auftrag der Bundesregierung. Migrationsbericht 2004. Nürnberg.

Federal Statistical Office (FSO) (2013a). *Bildung und Kultur.* Studierende an Hochschulen. Fachserie 11, Reihe 4.1. Wintersemester 2012/13. Wiesbaden.

Federal Statistical Office (FSO) (2013b). *Deutsche Studierende im Ausland.* Statistischer Überblick 2001-2011. Wiesbaden.

Federal Statistical Office (FSO) (2014). *Bevölkerung und Erwerbstätigkeit.* Ausländische Bevölkerung. Ergebnisse des Ausländerzentralregisters. Fachserie 1 Reihe 2. Wiesbaden.

Federal Statistical Office (FSO) (2014). *Bevölkerungsstatistik.* https://www.destatis.de/DE/ZahlenFakten/GesellschaftStaat/Bevoelkerung/Bev oelkerung.html

Finch, J. & Mason, J. (1993). *Negotiating family responsibilities.* London: Routledge.

Finch, T., Latorre, M., Pollard, N., Ruuter, J. (2009). *Shall we stay or shall we go? Remigration trends among Britain's immigrants.* London, Institute for Public Research.

Fincke, G. (2009). *Abgehängt, chancenlos, unwillig? Eine empirische Reorientierung von Integrationstheorien zu MigrantInnen der zweiten Generation in Deutschland.* Wiesbaden: VS Verlag.

Fleetwood, S. (2007). Why work–life balance now?. *The international journal of human resource management,* 18(3), 387-400.

Fokkema, T., Naderi, R. (2013). Differences in late-life loneliness: a comparison between Turkish and native-born older adults in Germany. *European Journal of Aging,* 10(4), 289-300.

Freeman, M.A. (2012). Nurse migration intentions in a Canadian border city.

Gangl, M. (2006). Scar effects of unemployment: An assessment of institutional complementarities. *American Sociological Review, 71*(6), 986-1013.

Gangl, M., & Ziefle, A. (2009). Motherhood, labor force behavior, and women's careers: An empirical assessment of the wage penalty for motherhood in Britain, Germany, and the United States. *Demography, 46*(2), 341-369.

Ganzeboom, H. B. G., de Graaf, P. M., & Treiman, D. J. (1992). A Standard International Socio-Economic Index of Occupational Status. *Social Science Research, 21,* 1-56.

German Academic Exchange Service (DAAD) and Deutsches Zentrum für Hochschul- und Wissenschaftsforschung (DZHW) (2013). *Wissenschaft Weltoffen* 2013. Online. http://www.wissenschaft-weltoffen.de/. [2014-10-05]

German Academic Exchange Service (Deutscher Akdamemischer Austauschdienst (DAAD) (2012). *Bildungsinländer 2011.* Daten und Fakten zur Situation von ausländischen Studierenden mit deutscher Hochschulzugangsberechtigung. Bonn.

Godbout, J. T. (1998). *The world of the gift.* Montreal, London: McGill- Queen's University Press.

Granato, N. (2003). *Ethnische Ungleichheit auf dem deutschen Arbeitsmarkt.* Opladen: Leske + Budrich.

Granovetter, M. S. (1973). The strength of weak ties. *American Journal of Sociology, 78*(6), 1360-1380.

Gray, B. (2008). Putting emotion and reflexivity to work in researching migration. *Sociology,* 42(5): 935–952.

Groenewold, G., &Lessard-Phillips, L. (2012). Research methodology. *Crul, M., Schneider, J., &Lelie, F. (eds) The European second generation compared. Does the integration context matter?* Amsterdam, Chicago: Amsterdam University Press, 39-56.

Grunow, D., Hofmeister, H., & Buchholz, S. (2006). Late 20th-century persistence and decline of the female homemaker in Germany and the United States. *International Sociology*, *21*(1), 101-131.

Gubrium, J. F. and J. A. Holstein (2009). *Analyzing Narrative Reality*. Los Angeles: Sage.

Güngor, N. D., & Tansel, A. (2007). *Brain drain form Turkey: An investigation of Students; Return Intentions.* ERC Working Papers in Economics 07/01. Ankara: Economic Research Center.

Hamel, C., Huschek, D., Milewski, N. & de Valk, H. (2012). Union formation and partner choice.*Crul, M., Schneider, J. &Lelie, F. (eds.) The European Second Generation Compared: Does the Integration Context Matter?* Amsterdam, Chicago: Amsterdam University Press, pp. 225-284.

Hanushek, E. A., Kain, J. F., Markman, J. M., & Rivkin, S. G. (2001). Does Peer Ability Affect Student Achievement? *National Bureau of Economic Research Working Paper Series, No. 8502.*

Haug, S. (2002). Familienstand, Schulbildung und Erwerbstätigkeit junger Erwachsener. Eine Analyse der ethnischen und geschlechtsspezifischen Ungleichheit – Erste Ergebnisse des Integrationssurveys des BiB. *Zeitschrift für Bevölkerungswissenschaft*, *27*(1), 115-144.

Haug, S. (2003). Interethnische Freundschaftsbeziehungen und soziale Integration. *Kölner Zeitschrift für Soziologie und Sozialpsychologie (KZfSS)*, *55*(4), 716-736.

Hawthorne, L. (2010). *Demography, migration and demand for international students.* In: Findlay, Christopher; Tierney, William G.: Globalisation and tertiary education in the Asia-Pacific. The changing nature of a dynamic market. Singapore.

Heath, A. F., Rothon, C., & Kilpi, E. (2008). The second generation in Western Europe: Education, unemployment, and occupational attainment. *Annual Review of Sociology*, *34*, 211-235.

Henn, A. & Koepping K.P. (eds.) (2008), *Rituals in an Unstable World: Contingency - Hybridity - Embodiment.* Frankfurt, Oxford: Lang Verlag.

Hoff Sommers, C. (1986). Filial morality. *The Journal of Philosophy,* 83: 439–456.

Hoff, E. (2006). How social contexts support and shape language development. *Developmental Review, 26,* 55-88.

Höhne, J., & Koopmans, R. (2010). *Host-country cultural capital and labour market trajectories of migrants in Germany: The impact of host-country orientation and migrant-specific human and social capital on labour market transitions* (No. SP IV 2010-701). Discussion papers//Wissenschaftszentrum Berlin für Sozialforschung (WZB), Research Unit Migration, Integration, Transnationalization.

Hortaçsu, N. (2007). Family- versus couple-initiated marriages in Turkey: Similarities and differences over the family life cycle. *Asian Journal of Social Psychology*, 10(2), 103-116.

Hummels, C., Overbeeke, C.J. & Klooster, S. (2007), Move to get moved: a search for methods, tools and knowledge to design for expressive and rich movement-based interaction. *Personal and Ubiquitous Computing*, volume 11, 8, 677-690.

Huschek, D., De Valk, H.A.G. &Liefbroer, A.C. (2012). Partner choice patterns among the descendants of Turkish immigrants in Europe. *European Journal of Population*, 28:241–268.

Huttenlocher, J., Haight, W., Bryk, A., Seltzer, M., & Lyons, T. (1991). Early Vocabulary Growth: Relation to Language Input and Gender. *Developmental Psychology, 27*, 236-248.

Inglehart, R. (1997). *Modernization and postmodernization: Cultural, economic, and political change in 43 societies*. Princeton, NJ: Princeton University Press.

Jennissen, R., Ooijevaar, J. & Nicolaas, H. (2014). Arbeidsmigratie. In: In R.P.W. Jennissen & H. Nicholaas (eds.). *De Nederlandse Migratiekaart 2013. Achtergronden en ontwikkelingen in internationale migratiestromen in de periode vanaf 2000.* Cahier 2014-8. Den Haag: WODC/CBS, p. 45-68.

Jong, G.F. de (2000). Expectations, gender and norms in migration decision- making. *Population Studies*, 54, 307-319.

Jong, G.F. de, & Fawcett, J.T. (1981). Motivations for migration: An assessment and a value-expectancy research model. In G.F. de Jong & R.W. Gardner (red.), *Migration decision making: Multidisciplinary approaches to micro level studies in developed and developing countries* (pp.13-58). NewYork: Pergamon Press.

Jong, G.F. de, Abad, R.G., Arnold, F., Cariño, B.V., Fawcett, J.T., & Gardner, R.W. (1983). International and internal migration decision making: A value-expectancy based analytical framework of intentions to move from a rural Philippine Province. *International Migration Review*, 17(3), 470-484.

Jong, G.F. de, Johnson, A.G., & Richter, K. (1996). Determinants of migration values and expectations in rural Thailand. *Asian and Pacific Migration Journal*. 5(4), 399-416.

Joseph, S. (1993). Gender and Relationality among Arab Families in Lebanon. *Feminist Studies,* 19(3): 465–486.

Kagitçibasi, Ç, &Ataca, B. (2005). Value of children and family change: A three-decade portrait from Turkey. *Applied Psychology*, 54(3) [Special Issue: Factors Influencing Value of Children and Intergenerational Relations in Times of Social Change: Analyses From Psychological and Socio-Cultural Perspectives], 317-337.

Kalanj, R. (2008). Modernizacija i identitet [Modernization and identity]. Zagreb, Politička kultura (in Croatian)

Kalmijn, M. (1994). Assortative mating by cultural and economic occupational status. *American Journal of Sociology*, 100(2), 422-452.

Kalmijn, M. (1998). Intermarriage and homogamy: Causes, patterns, trends. *Annual Review of Sociology*, 24(1), 395-421.

Kalter, F. (2006). Auf der Suche nach einer Erklärung für die spezifischen Arbeitsmarktnachteile Jugendlicher türkischer Herkunft. Zugleich eine Replik auf den Beitrag von Holger Seibert und Heike Solga:" Gleiche Chancen dank

FAMILY AND HUMAN CAPITAL IN TURKISH MIGRATION

einer abgeschlossenen Ausbildung?"(ZfS 5/2005). *Zeitschrift für Soziologie,* *35*(2), 144-160.

Kalter, F., & Granato, N. (2002). Recent Trends of Assimilation in Germany. *ZUMA – Arbeitsbericht 2001/02.*

Kanas, A., Chiswick, B. R., Lippe, T., & Tubergen, F. (2012). Social contacts and the economic performance of immigrants: A panel study of immigrants in Germany. *International Migration Review, 46*(3), 680-709.

Karakaşoğlu, Y. (2012). Bildung und Erziehung. In: Steinbach, U. (Hrsg.),*Länderbericht Türkei*. Bonn, Bundeszentrale für politische Bildung, S. 286-305.

Kerpelman, J. L., & Schvaneveldt, P. L. (1999). Young adults' anticipated identity importance of career, marital, and parental roles: Comparisons of men and women with different role balance orientations. Sex Roles, 41, 189–217.

Kint, J., Ross, P. & Overbeeke, C.J. (2010). D'Ou venons nous? Que sommes nous? Ou allons nous? *Keer International Conference on Kansei Engineering and Emotion Research*, Paris, 1-10.

Klaver J., Stouten, J., & van der Welle, I. (2010). *Emigratie uit Nederland. Een verkennende studie naar de emigratiemotieven van hoger opgeleiden.* Amsterdam, Regioplan.

Klein, W. & Dimroth, C. (2003). Expertisen zu grundlegenden Fragen. *IMIS-Beiträge, 21,* 127-161.

Klooster, S. & Overbeeke, C. J. (2005). Designing products as an integral part of choreography of interaction: the product's form as an integral part of movement. *Proc. of the 1st European Workshop on Design and Semantics of Form and Movement.* Newcastle, UK, 23-35.

Köbrich Leon, A. (2013). *Does cultural heritage affect employment decisions: Empirical evidence for second generation immigrants in Germany* (No. 270). University of Lüneburg Working Paper Series in Economics.

König, S., & Cesinger, B. (2015). Gendered work–family conflict in Germany: do self-employment and flexibility matter?. Work, Employment & Society, 0950017014545264.

Kohler, M., Rieck, A., Borch, S., & Ziese, T. (2005). *Erster telefonischer Gesundheitssurvey des Robert Koch-Instituts – Methodische Beiträge. [First phone survey of the Robert Koch-Institute – Methodical contributions.]* Berlin (in German).

Kristen, C., & Granato, N. (2007). The educational attainment of the second generation in Germany. *Ethnicities, 7*(3), 343-366.

Kulu-Glasgow, I. , Schans D., Smit M., Vleugel M.J., & Uitterhoeve J. Met medewerking van Boersema E., & Chotkowski. M. (2014). *Gezocht: buitenlandse toptalent. Evaluatie van de Regeling Hoogopgeleiden.* Cahier 2014-4. Den Haag: WODC.

Kwak, K. (2003). Adolescents and their parents: A review of intergenerational family relations for immigrant and non-immigrant families. *Human Development*, 46(2-3), 115 - 136.

Lancee, B. (2012). The economic returns of bonding and bridging social capital for immigrant men in Germany. *Ethnic and Racial Studies*, *35*(4), 664-683.

Leavitt, J. (1996). Meaning and feeling in the anthropology of emotions. *American Ethnologist*, 23(3): 514–539.

Liljeström, R. & Özdalga, E. (eds) (2002). *Autonomy and dependence in the family: Turkey and Sweden in critical perspective.* Istanbul: Swedish Research Institute.

Lucassen, J., & Penninx, R. (1997). *Newcomers: Immigrants and their Descendants in the Netherlands 1550-1995.* Amsterdam: Het Spinhuis.

Luthra, R. R. (2013). Explaining ethnic inequality in the German labor market: labor market institutions, context of reception, and boundaries. *European sociological review*, 29(5), 1095-1107.

Martin, P.L. and Sirkeci, I. (2015). Introduction. In: Sirkeci, I., Elcin, D., and Seker, G. (Eds.). *Politics and Law in Turkish Migration.* London: Transnational Press London, pp. 1-6.

Maxwell, R. (2010). Evaluating Migrant Integration: Political Attitudes across Generations in Europe. *International Migration Review.* 44 (1), 25–52.

McMaster University. Open Access Dissertations and Theses. Paper 6900. www.digitalcommons.mcmaster.ca/cgi/viewcontent.cgi?article=7939&context= op endissertations.

Mendelsohn, A. L., Brockmeyer, C. A., Dreyer, B. P., Fierman, A. H., Berkule-Silberman, S. B., & Tomopoulos, S. (2010). Do Verbal Interactions with Infants During Electronic Media Exposure Mitigate Adverse Impacts on their Language Development as Toddlers? *Infant and Child Development, 19,* 577-593.

Mesić, M. (2006). Multikulturalizam. Društveni i teorijski izazovi [Multiculturalism]. Zagreb, Školska knjiga (in Croatian)

Milewski, N. (2011). Transition to a first birth among Turkish second-generation migrants in Western Europe. *Advances in Life Course Research, 16*(4), 178-189.

Milewski, N., & Hamel, C. (2010). Union formation and partner choice in a transnational context: The case of descendants of Turkish immigrants in France. *International Migration Review,* 44(3), 615–658.

Milewski, N., & Kulu, H. (2014).Why have mixed couples a high risk of divorce: Immigrant-native marriages in Germany. *European Journal of Population*, 30(1), 89-113.

Milewski, N. (2007). First child of immigrant workers and their descendants in West Germany: Interrelation of events, disruption, or adaptation? *Demographic Research* 17(29), 859–896. www.demographic-research.org/Volumes/Vol17/29/17-29.pdf.

Milewski, N. (2013). Erwerbsbeteiligung und Einstellungen zur Familie von türkischen Migrantinnen im Generationenvergleich (Labour force participation and family attitudes of first and second generation Turkish migrant women). *Zeitschrift für Familienforschung* (Journal of Family Research) 25(1), 53-74.

145

Milewski, N.; Doblhammer, G. (2015). Mental health among immigrants: Is there a disadvantage in later life? In: Doblhammer, G. (Ed.): Health among the elderly in Germany: New evidence on disease, disability and care need. Series on Population Studies by the Federal Institute for Population Research, Vol. 46, Opladen, Berlin, Toronto: Barbara Budrich, 191-212.

Mincer, J. (1974). *Schooling, Experience, and Earnings*. New York: Columbia University Press.

Munniksma, A., Flache, A., Verkuyten, M., &Veenstra, R. (2012). Parental acceptance of children's intimate ethnic outgroup relations: The role of culture, status, and family reputation. *International Journal of Intercultural Relations*, 36(4), 575-585.

Muttarak, R. (2010). Explaining trends and patterns of immigrants' partner choice in Britain.*ZeitschriftfürFamilienforschung/Journalof Family Research*, 22(1), 37-64.

Naldemirci, Ö. (2003). *Caring (in) diaspora: Aging and caring experiences of older Turkish migrants in a Swedish context*. Unpublished doctoral dissertation, University of Gothenburg.

Nauck, B. & Suckow, J. (2002). Soziale Netzwerke und Generationen beziehungenim interkulturellen Vergleich. Soziale Beziehungen von Müttern und Großmüttern in Japan, Korea, China, Indonesien, Israel, Deutschland und der Türkei. *ZeitschriftfürSoziologie der Erziehung und Sozialisation, 22(4)*, 374-392.

Nauck, B., & Klaus, D. (2008). Family change in Turkey: peasant society, Islam and the revolution "from above". *Jayakody, R., Thornton, A., and Axinn, W. G. (eds.) International family change*. Ideational perspectives.New York, Oxon: Taylor & Francis, 281-312.

Nauck, B., Kohlmann, A., & Diefenbach, H. (1997). FamiliäreNetzwerke, intergenerative Transmission und Assimilationsprozessebeitürkischen Migrantenfamilien. *KölnerZeitschriftfürSoziologie und Sozialpsychologie*, 49(3), 477-499.

Nauck, B. (1985). „Heimliches Matriarchat" in Familien türkischer Arbeitsmigranten? Empirische Ergebnisse zu Veränderungen der Entscheidungsmacht und Aufgabenallokation. *Zeitschrift für Soziologie,14, 6*, S. 450-465.

Nauck, B. & Suckow, J. (2002). Soziale Netzwerke und Generationenbeziehungen im interkulturellen Vergleich. Soziale Beziehungen von Müttern und Großmüttern in Japan, Korea, China, Indonesien, Israel, Deutschland und der Türkei. *Zeitschrift für Soziologie der Erziehung und Sozialisation22, 4*, S.374-392.

Nicolaas, H., Liu, J. & de Boer, S. (2011). Gezinsmigratie. In R.P.W Jennissen (red). *De Nederlandse migratiekaart: Achtergronden en ontwikkelingen van verschillende internationale migratietypen*. Den Haag: Boom Juridische uitgevers. Onderzoek en beleid 299, pp. 149-175.

Nummela, O., Sulander, T., Helakorpi, S., Haapola, I., Uutela, A., Heinonen, H., Valve, R. & Fogelholm, M. (2011). Register-based data indicated nonparticipation bias in a health study among aging people. *Journal of clinical epidemiology*, *64*(12), 1418–1425.

Obradović, E. (2013). *Monitor kennismigranten: Kwantitatieve Analyse*. Den Haag: IND.

Obradović, E. (2014). *Monitor kennismigranten: Kwalitatieve analyse*. Den Haag: IND.

OECD (2013a). *Recruiting Immigrant Workers: Germany*. OECD Publishing. Paris.

OECD (2013b). *Education at a glance 2013: OECD Indicators*. OECD Publishing. Paris.

Oswald, I. (2007). Migrationssoziologie [Migration sociology]. Konstanz, UVK (in German)

Paas, T., Eamets, R., Masso, J., & Rõõm, M. (2003). Labour Market Flexibility and Migration in the Baltic States: Macro Evidences. *University of Tartu-Faculty of Economics & Business Administration Working Paper Series*, (16).

Pan, B. A., Rowe, M., Singer, J. D., & Snow, C. E. (2005). Maternal Correlates of Growth in Toddler Vocabulary Production in Low-Income Families. *Child Development, 76*, 763-782.

Park, H., Tsai, K. M., Liu, L. L., & Lau, A. S. (2012). Transactional associations between supportive family climate and young children's heritage language proficiency in immigrant families. *International Journal of Behavioral Development, 36*, 226-236.

Peters, P., Den Dulk, L., & van der Lippe, T. (2009). The effects of time-spatial flexibility and new working conditions on employees' work–life balance: The Dutch case. *Community, Work & Family*, 12(3), 279-297.

Peterson, A. (2005). *Engendering emotions*. New York: Palgrave Macmillan.

Piore, M., & Doeringer, P. (1971). *Internal labor markets and manpower analysis*. Lexington, Mass.: DC Heath.

Pries, L. (2010). *Transnationalisierung. Theorie und Empirie grenzüberschreitender Vergesellschaftung*. Wiesbaden: VS VerlagfürSozialwissenschaften.

Qin, D. B. (2006). Our child doesn't talk to us anymore: Alienation in immigrant Chinese families. *Anthropology & Education Quarterly*, 37(2), 167-179.

Rappaport, R.A. (1999). *Ritual and Religion in the Making of Humanity*, Cambridge University Press, Cambridge Mass.

Razum, O.; Twardella, D. (2002): Time travel with Oliver Twist. Towards an explanation for a paradoxically low mortality among recent immigrants. In *Tropical Medicine & International Health* 7(1), pp. 4-9.

Reckwitz, A. (2008). Unscharfe Grenzen. Perspektiven der Kultursoziologie [Blurred boundaries]. Bielefeld, Transcript Verlag (in German)

Reed-Danahay, D.E. (1997). Introduction, in D.E. Reed-Danahay (ed), *Auto-Ethnography: Rewriting the Self and the Social*, Berg, Oxford, 1-17.

Reilly, P. (2001). *Flexibility at Work: Balancing the interests of employers and employee*. Hampshire: Gower Publishing Limited.

Renzaho, A.M.N., McCabe, M., & Sainsbury, W.J. (2011). Parenting, role reversals and the preservation of cultural values among Arabic speaking migrant families in Melbourne, Australia. *International Journal ofIntercultural Relations*, 35(4), 416-424.

Richtermoc, M. (2014). Über die Selbstbestimmung und den Integrationsstand der Jugendliche der 2. Und 3. Generation mit türkischem Herkunft in Wien. Unpublished master thesis. University of Zagreb (in German)

Ricoeur, P. (1984). *Time and narrative*. Chicago: The University of Chicago Press

Robert Koch Institut (Ed.) (2008). *Schwerpunktbericht der Gesundheitsberichterstattung des Bundes: Migration und Gesundheit. [Focus report offered by the Federal Health Monitoring information system: Migration and Health.]* Berlin (in German).

Robinson, W. I. (2009). Saskia Sassen and the sociology of globalization: A critical appraisal. *Sociological Analysis*, 3(1), 5-29.

Sammons, P., Elliot, K., Sylva, K., Melhuish, E., Siraj-Blatchford, I., & Taggart, B. (2004). The Impact of Pre-school on Young Children's Cognitive Attainments at Entry to Reception. *British Educational Research Journal, 30,* 691-712.

Sassen, S. (1988). *The Mobility of Capital and Labor: A Study in International Investment and Labor Flow*. Cambridge: Cambridge University Press.

Sassen, S. (1998). *Globalization and its Discontents: Essays on the New Mobility of People and Money*. New York: The New Press.

Schenk, L., & Neuhauser, H. (2005). Beteiligung von Migranten im telefonischen Gesundheitssurvey. [Participation of migrants in the phone health survey.] *Gesundheitswesen, 67,* 719–725 (in German).

Schultz, T.W. (1961). Investment in Human Capital. *The American Economic Review*, 51 (1), 1-17.

Schwartz, R.L. (1996). Body, Space and Idea. The Connected Body? *Allsopp, R. & deLahunta, S., (eds.) An Interdisciplinary Approach to the Body and Performance Amsterdam: Amsterdam School of the Arts, pp. 77-81.*

Seibert, H. (2011). Berufserfolg von jungen Erwachsenen mit Migrationshintergrund. Wie Ausbildungsabschlüsse, ethnische Herkunft und ein deutscher Pass die Arbeitsmarktchancen beeinflussen. In Becker, R. (Ed.). *Integration durch Bildung* pp. 197-226. Wiesbaden: VS Verlag für Sozialwissenschaften.

Sengenberger, W. (1987). *Struktur und Funktionsweise von Arbeitsmärkten: Die Bundesrepublik Deutschland im internationalen Vergleich*. Frankfurt/Main: Campus Verlag.

Sirkeci, I., Cohen, J.H. and Yazgan, P. (2012). The Turkish culture of migration: Flows between Turkey and Germany, socio-economic development and conflict. *Migration Letters*, 9(1):33-46.

Sirkeci, I., Cohen, J., and Ratha, D. (eds.) (2012). *Migration and Remittances during the Global Financial Crisis and Beyond*. Washington, DC. USA: The World Bank.

Skrbiš, Z. (2008). Transnational families: Theorizing migration, emotions and belonging. *Journal of Intercultural Studies*, 29(3): 231–246.

Skrbiš, Z. and Svašek, M. (2007). Passions and powers: Emotions and globalization. *Identities: Global Studies in Culture and Power*, 14: 367–383.

Sluzki, C.E. (1979): Migration and family conflict. In *Family Process* 18(4), pp. 379-390.

Soehl, T., & Yahirun, J. (2011). Timing of union formation and partner choice in immigrant societies: The United States and Germany. *Advances in Life Course Research*, *16*(4), 205-216.

Stark, O. and Taylor, J.E. (1989). Relative deprivation and international migration. *Demography*, 26: 1-14.

Statistische Ämter des Bundes und der Länder (2014). *Gemeindeverzeichnis. Gebiets-stand: 31.12.2013. [List of municipalities. Territorial status: 31.12.2013].* Retrieved from www.destatis.de/DE/ ZahlenFakten/Laender Regionen/Regionales/Gemeindeverzeichnis/Administrativ/Archiv/GVAuszugQ /AuszugGV4QAktuell.html (in German).

Statistisches Bundesamt (2014a). *Bevölkerung und Erwerbstätigkeit: Ausländische Bevölkerung. [Population and occupation: Foreign population.]* Retrieved from www.destatis.de/ DE/Publikationen/ Thematisch/ Bevoelkerung /MigrationIntegration/AuslaendBevoelkerung.html (in German).

Statistisches Bundesamt (2014b). *GENSESIS-Online Datenbank. [GENESIS-Online database].* Retrieved from www-genesis.destatis.de (in German).

Storper et al. (2009). Rethinking human capital, creativity and urban growth. *Journal of Economic Geography,* 9 (2), 147-167.

Straßburger, G. (2003). *Heiratsverhalten und Partnerwahlim Einwanderungs kontext. Eheschließungen der zweiten Migranten generation türkischer Herkunft.* Würzburg: ErgonVerlag (Doctoral Thesis).

Sunata, U. (2011). Highly skilled labor migration: the case of ICT specialists from Turkey in Germany. LIT Verlag Münster.

Sussman, M.B., 1953. Parental participation in mate selection and its effect upon family continuity.*Social Forces*, 32(1), 76-81.

Svašek, M. (2008). Who cares? Families and feelings in movement. *Journal of Intercultural Studies*, 29(3): 213–230.

Svašek, M. (2010). On the move: Emotions and human mobility. *Journal of Ethnic and Migration Studies,* 36(6): 865–880.

Teule, J., Vanderwaeren, E. & Mbah-Fongkimeh, A. (2012). *Marriage migration from Emirdağ to Brussels.* Brussels: King Baudouin Foundation.

The New Oxford Dictionary of English (ed.) (2001). Oxford University Press

Thode, N.; Bergmann, E.; Kamtsiuris, P. & Kurth B.M. (2005). Einflussfaktoren auf die ambulante Inanspruchnahme in Deutschland. [Factors influencing ambulant utilisation in Germany]. *Bundesgesundheitsblatt 48,* 296–306 (in German).

Timmerman, C. & al. (2009). Marriage at the intersection between tradition and globalization, *History of the Family* 14 (2), 232 -244.

149

Titzmann, P. (2012). Growing up too soon? Parentification among immigrant and native adolescents in Germany. *Journal of Youth and Adolescence*, 41(7), 880-893.

Tomopoulos, S., Dreyer, B. P., Berkule, S., Fierman, A. H., Brockmeyer, C., & Mendelsohn, A. L. (2010). Infant media exposure and toddler development. *Arch Pediatr Adolesc Med, 164,* 1105-1111.

Topgül, C. (2015). Family influence on partner choice of second generation: What are the experiences of Turkish origin women in Switzerland? *Aybek, C., Huinink, J., &Muttarak, R. (eds.) Spatial Mobility, Migration, and Family Dynamics.* Dordrecht: Springer, 43-66.

Tronto, J. (1993). *Moral boundaries: A Political argument for an ethic of care.* New York, London: Routledge.

Ulram, P. (2009). Integration in Österreich. Einstellungen, Orientierungen und Erfahrungen von MigrantInnen und Angehörigen der Mehrheitsbevölkerung [Integration in Austria]. Vienna, GfK/BMI (in German)

United Nations Educational, Scientific and Cultural Organization (UNESCO) Institute for Statistics (2014). *Global flow of tertiary-level students.* Online. http://www.uis.unesco.org/Education/Pages/international-student-flow-viz.aspx [2015-01-08]

Van Gennep, A. (1977). *The Rites of Passage.* London, UK: Routledge, & Kegan Paul. (Original work published 1909).

Van Huis, M. (2007). Partnerkeuze van allochtonen. Bevolkingstrends, 4e kwartaal 2007. CBS, p. 25-31.

Van Zantvliet, P.I., Kalmijn, M. &Verbakel, E. (2014). Parental involvement in partner choice: The case of Turks and Moroccans in the Netherlands. *Journal of Ethnic and Migration Studies*, 30(3), 387-398.

Vandello, J. A., Hettinger, V. E., Bosson, J. K., & Siddiqi, J. (2013). When equal isn't really equal: The masculine dilemma of seeking work flexibility. Journal of Social Issues, 69(2), 303-321.

Wallace, C. (2003). Work Flexibility in Eight European countries: A cross-national comparison. *Sociological Series 60.* Vienna: Institute for Advanced Studies.

Wentzel M., Viljoen, J., & Kok, P. (2006). Contemporary South African migration patterns and intentions. In P. Kok, D. Gelderblom, J.O. Oucho & J. van Zyl (red), *Migration in South and Southern Africa: Dynamics and determinants* (pp. 171-204). Chicago: Independent Publishers Group.

White, M.J. and Lindstrom, D.P. (2006). Internal migration. In: *Handbook of Population*, D.L. Poston and M. Micklin (eds.). Springer: Texas, pp. 311-346.

Wilde, D. Schiphorst & T. Klooster, S. (2011). Move to Design, Design to Move: a conversation about designing for the body. *ACM Interactions Magazine*, 18 (4), 22 -27.

Wilkinson C., Goedvolk, M., & van Dieten, S. (2008). Korte termijn-evaluatie Wet inburgering buitenland. Barneveld: Significant.

WODC/INDIAC (2009). *Internationale gezinsvorming begrensd? Een evaluatie van de gevolgen van de verhoging van de inkomens- en leeftijdseis bij migratie van buitenlandse partners naar Nederland.* The Hague: WODC, Cahier 2009-4.

Xiao, J. (2001). *Determinants of salary growth in Shenzhen China: An analysis of formal education, on-the-job training, and adult education with a three-level model.* Chinese University of Hong Kong.

Yavuz, S. (2008). *Fertility decline in Turkey from the 1980s onwards: Patterns by main language groups.* Ankara: HUIPS [Doctoral Thesis].

Zeyneloğlu, S., & Sirkeci, İ. (2014). Türkiye'de Almanlar ve Almancılar. *Göç Dergisi*, 1(1), 77-118. http://tplondon.com/dergi/index.php/gd/article/view/5.

www.ingramcontent.com/pod-product-compliance
Lightning Source LLC
Chambersburg PA
CBHW020706270326
41928CB00005B/288